PRAISE FOR *MODERN MANAGER*

"Powerful, empathic and actionable. Buy a copy for your boss, or even better, for yourself."
—Seth Godin, author of *This is Marketing*

"Corina Walsh highlights the frustrations of the first-time manger in her new book *Modern Manager*. I wish there had been a resource like this when I first entered the ranks of management. You will clearly see the most talented leaders lead based on a rock-solid foundation of clear and basic human values. As a leader you will be tested and even frustrated. This book will help you build the resilience and skills you need to get the job done and become a successful modern leader."
—Pattie Lovett-Reid, former chief financial commentator, CTV News

"Clear, precise, and actionable . . . *Modern Manager* is a savvy, insightful leadership guide to effective, humancentric management."
—*Foreword* Clarion Reviews

"This book was practical and occasionally counterintuitive. It intelligently challenged and deconstructed commonly held sacred cows of managerial wisdom. Corina Walsh strikes a great balance between explaining the new realities of managing in the post-covid era and providing practical instruction on how to 'become the change' managers are seeking from their teams."

—Emad Rizkalla, founder and CEO, Bluedrop

"As a first-time CEO of a tech startup, I wanted to build a culture and team unlike the legacy corporate environments I had experienced. My goal was to create a modern company that was highly productive, fulfilling, and a joy to work at. This of course was going to require strong, modern leadership throughout the organization. In *Modern Manager*, Corina Walsh provides an engaging, story-filled exploration of the core principles of her leadership development programs, which have been crucial to our success in creating a high-performing, people-first culture."

—Joshua Green, cofounder and CEO, Mysa

"In the modern, technology-enabled workplace, a manager's ability to direct, delegate, develop, coach, and empower their employees is more important than ever. I read *Modern Manager* looking for tips to support new managers on our team and young entrepreneurs managing employees for the first time. Corina's insightful illustrations, exercises, tools, and reminders are a fantastic resource for beginner managers—and are just as relevant for experienced managers looking to improve. This is a great book to help managers of all tenures hone and refresh their skills to create an environment where employees excel and organizations thrive."

—Karen Greve Young, CEO, Futurpreneur

"Finally, a book that acknowledges the demanding yet profoundly influential role of people managers, especially in the current challenging times. Corina reveals the essential skills that turn typical managerial frustrations into highly effective people-management practices. In so doing, she elevates the importance of people managers and advocates for organizations to take their development seriously. *Modern Manager* is not just a theoretical guide but a practical tool kit for bolstering our capacity to develop, coach, and enable the people we lead. Chock full of tried-and-true wisdom from the author's considerable experience, it is a book managers and people developers will find themselves returning to often. I know I will."

—Dr. Brenda Barker Scott, organizational design expert and former faculty member, Queen's University IRC

"Corina Walsh's book reminds us once again our role as leaders is to create the space for people to learn, practice, and build the skills that empower teams and to close the gap that occurs when people are not well prepared or well supported in their roles as leaders. By understanding the five frustrations of leadership, and sharing valuable tools to help mitigate their impact, Corina has written a book that is both informative and practical in applying knowledge and shaping better leaders for our future."

—Molly Kurth, SVP, learning and talent development, Compass Group

Modern Manager

Modern Manager

CONQUERING THE FIVE FRUSTRATIONS OF LEADERSHIP

Corina Walsh

GFB

Copyright © 2025 by Corina Walsh

All rights reserved.

No part of this book may be reproduced, or stored in a retrieval system, or transmitted in any form or by any means, electronic, mechanical, photocopying, recording, or otherwise, without express written permission of the publisher.

Published by GFB™, Seattle
www.girlfridayproductions.com

Produced by Girl Friday Productions

Cover design: Emily Weigel
Production editorial: Katherine Richards
Project management: Emilie Sandoz-Voyer

ISBN (paperback): 978-1-959411-83-3
ISBN (ebook): 978-1-959411-84-0

Library of Congress Control Number: 2024909396

First edition

*To Derrick and Dylan, who show me
every day how to lead and live with joy*

*To the leaders who embrace the
challenges of modern management*

Contents

Foreword xiii
Introduction 1
Chapter 1
    How Did We Get Here? 15
Chapter 2
    Frustration #1—Micromanagement Misunderstanding . . . 29
Chapter 3
    Frustration #2—Delegation Disappointment 47
Chapter 4
    Frustration #3—Feedback Fiasco 71
Chapter 5
    Frustration #4—Coaching Confusion 112
Chapter 6
    Frustration #5—Motivation Mismatch 137
Conclusion
    The Critical Path Forward for Managers 165
Appendix A
    Filling the Leadership Pipeline from Within 177
Appendix B
    Making the Case for Leadership Development 187

Notes 191
About the Author 195

Foreword

Traditional paradigms of leadership have been irrevocably altered in the wake of the pandemic. Much of the prepandemic leadership wisdom was tailored to a world that no longer exists. The disruption we're experiencing is profound and ongoing, and within this upheaval lies an unparalleled opportunity for growth and transformation. *Modern Manager* is the blueprint for companies and leaders as they navigate the journey ahead.

The shift toward a four-day workweek reflects employees' desire for better work-life balance. Trusting employees, implementing the right processes, and setting appropriate guardrails and key performance indicators can result in a more productive, successful, and satisfied workforce. Moreover, in an era increasingly dominated by artificial intelligence and other technology, soft skills and emotional intelligence have emerged as critical assets.

The presence of women in key leadership roles is on the rise, and achieving gender equality is crucial for harnessing the full potential of our collective skills and navigating this new reality. We cannot cling to outdated methods while expecting different results; we must embrace positive change and strive for a more equal society. This includes providing constructive feedback, communicating effectively with a diverse workforce, and understanding the unique contributions of different generations. Mastering these skills is vital for managers to succeed in today's dynamic and evolving work environment.

Time is our most valuable asset—acquiring it, saving it, and creating more of it in our lives has become paramount. Modern managers require tools to lead teams efficiently and effectively to focus on what truly matters.

In *Modern Manager: Conquering the Five Frustrations of Leadership*, Corina Walsh offers a timely and indispensable resource for managers at every level. The expectations of the workforce have changed dramatically, and leaders now require a broad array of skills to manage diverse, multigenerational teams, often in remote work settings. The stakes have never been higher, and Corina has captured practical, actionable strategies and tools for leading teams effectively. This book is an essential guide for the managers who will steer your organization through these disruptive yet exhilarating times.

—Jennifer Gillivan, ICD.D, president and CEO of the IWK Foundation, recipient of Waterstone Human Capital's 2023 Canada's Most Admired CEO award

INTRODUCTION

Why the Frustration You're Feeling Isn't Your Fault (and Why It's Fixable)

What would you say if I asked you to build your house on a shaky foundation? That would be a hard no! Unfortunately, the leadership journey of many managers is built on unstable footing. Most managers are promoted because they were strong individual performers and are in their first management role for ten years before they receive training[1]. When a manager is in their role without proper training for an extended period, the likelihood that they will develop negative habits for leading based on coping instead of thriving increases dramatically. It also increases the chances they will pass on bad habits to newer managers they may be mentoring. This vicious cycle creates an unstable leadership foundation throughout the entire company, impacting the careers and well-being of employees and managers.

I started my leadership development business in 2015 because I wanted to help high-growth, technology, and knowledge-based companies understand how to engage their employees. Each year I collected data points on the experiences of managers registering for my programs. Overwhelmingly, managers wrote that they were frustrated and even slightly burned out from dealing with the "people stuff" without the tools and skills they need to be effective.

What has become clear from training and coaching hundreds of managers over the years is that most don't necessarily understand why being a manager is so challenging in the first place. First-time managers are often still basking in the glow of their first promotion when they are faced with the reality that being responsible for the performance of a team is very different from being responsible for your own performance. I've heard the same story countless times during chance encounters with people. Whether I'm at a coffee shop or on an airplane, it's become almost comical how frequently this topic arises when someone asks about my profession. The person next to me will ask what I do for a living. "I am a leadership coach," I respond. "I help new managers who were promoted because of their technical skill gain the people-management skills they need to lead a team." The response from the other person is always the same. "Let me tell you about the first time I was promoted to management! I was doing well as an individual performer on the team, so they promoted me to manager of that team. I was a peer and then I became responsible for leading the team. Some of my team members were not happy, and I received no support from my own manager. It was a disaster."

I dream of the day when I hear a different story. It might sound like this: "I received my first promotion to management after several lengthy conversations with our people and culture manager and the director of the department. They asked me if I was interested in a people-management role. We evaluated my skills, including my people-management skills, to identify areas where I might need to improve. We also had conversations on what being a first-time manager would look like and what I should expect. I accepted the role with my eyes wide open. I participated in new-manager training sessions and received ongoing guidance from an internal mentor who had undergone similar training, providing invaluable insights on overcoming challenges. My team members expressed excitement about working with me, and I felt good about the opportunity." While I have yet to hear a story like this from anyone, I take comfort in the fact that I am working with companies each year that are dedicated to learning how to effectively promote and prepare new managers.

Promoting a strong individual performer to a management position without providing expectations and necessary training for success is cruel. New and experienced managers require tools and support to be effective in their role. The same skills that make someone a rock-star individual performer are not enough to help them succeed as a manager.

I wrote this book because I am tired of hearing the same version of the first time–manager horror story repeatedly. This book aims to help managers, executives, and business owners realize the root cause of their frustrations, what aspects they have control and influence over, and what they can do about it to ease their pain.

THE FIVE CORE FRUSTRATIONS OF MANAGERS

This book examines the five core frustrations most managers are struggling with, including the root cause of each frustration (spoiler: it's rarely coming from your direct report), and provides tools and strategies to overcome each frustration, including:

1. why a fear of being labeled a micromanager leads to most managers not managing enough;
2. why managers delegate but still don't get what they need from their direct reports and end up taking the work back and doing it themselves;
3. why managers avoid delivering constructive feedback, and why most employees do not use the feedback they receive;
4. why managers are not utilizing coaching effectively to support employees to improve their performance, what it means to coach an employee for performance, and how to know what questions to ask next; and
5. why most efforts to motivate and engage employees do not work, and what today's employees need to feel inspired.

New managers typically encounter challenges with delegating, delivering constructive feedback, and finding a comfort level with ensuring deliverables are met without micromanaging. Other challenges include navigating the transition of moving from peer to supervisor, leading people who are older and have more experience, and leading a team when the manager doesn't have the technical expertise of the team. Overwhelmed hardworking managers often proclaim, "But I am delegating!" or "I did give them feedback!" There is a tendency for a manager to blame the employee for these issues if they have not received guidance on what to expect when in their new role or management training. The lack of understanding as to why these frustrations are occurring creates tension between the employee and their manager.

During a typical Canadian snowstorm, I noticed the college students renting the house across the street were attempting to remove a large boulder of snow from their driveway with a hockey stick! Once I stopped laughing, I realized the obvious lesson we could all learn: you are only as good as your tools. You could be the best person in the world, but without the right tools and skills, you may never be the most effective manager you could be. Most managers who come through my programs don't even realize there are tools to help you manage a team. They would often express their struggles to their HR manager, a colleague, or a spouse who had heard about my programs and suggested they enroll. Leading a team without the tools, skills, and knowledge you need reduces your resilience, affects the engagement and motivation of your team, and impedes productivity and growth. Not to mention the impact it can have on your own career. So, before you question whether you are cut out for management, ask yourself if you have the tools, knowledge, and support a manager needs to succeed.

EASING THE FRUSTRATION OF LEADING STARTS HERE

When I started my business in 2015, workplaces looked very different. There was no pandemic threatening to permanently change how and where we work. The remote-work option was still on the wish list for most knowledge workers. Artificial intelligence was in the R&D phase and not a mainstream tool used daily by companies and employees.

There is, however, one core aspect of our work that has not undergone a drastic change—employee engagement levels. The percentage of employees considered engaged in the United States in 2023 was hovering at 33 percent—a nominal increase from 32 percent in 2015.[2]

Before starting my business, I changed jobs three times in search of a company that understood the importance of engaging its workforce. I began each job enthusiastically and eager to contribute through my knowledge and skills.

Inevitably, each role would end with me feeling discouraged and disengaged for reasons you can read about in my first book, *The Engaged Employee Blueprint: Build a Workplace Culture Where Employees Thrive*. I would move on to another organization, hoping for a different culture and a different type of manager.

With each new organization, I noticed that my colleagues were similar. Most were moderately engaged. They enjoyed their work and were good at it but were struggling with the same obstacles I encountered, such as dealing with layers of management, ineffective communication channels, and a negative workplace culture.

I knew there had to be a solution. Over time, I recognized

the complexity of the demands my previous directors and executives faced, and my empathy for their challenges grew. By then, I had extensive experience and clear strategies for how companies and managers could finally understand how to engage their employees.

One pandemic and many clients later, my work has evolved into a specialization in leadership development designed to change the way both managers and employees interact with each other.

When completing the research for my first book, I found a startling statistic. In its *State of the American Manager: Analytics and Advice for Leaders* report, Gallup states that "managers account for at least 70% of the variance in employee engagement scores across business units."

All this time, I had been talking to companies about anything and everything that might make their workplaces better for the people working there. I delivered sessions on the importance of recognition, providing professional development opportunities to employees, improving communication within the company, and taking the pulse of your workforce. I wasn't focusing on the most important relationship that impacted how an employee feels when they show up for work each day—their relationship with their own manager.

Of course, it's the manager! Think about it. Who has the most influence over and impact on an employee's career trajectory? Who will affect how an employee feels when they show up for work each day? We are all familiar with the adage "People don't quit jobs; they quit managers." While I don't think this is always the case and puts unfair pressure on the average manager, there is no doubt that an employee's relationship with their manager has a huge influence on how they experience the culture of that organization and their day-to-day work lives.

With this realization, I began offering one-on-one leadership coaching and training on various management topics. It didn't take long to realize that most managers and executives I worked with had the same problems, and I began collecting data points on their experiences. Most managers struggled in the same areas and didn't have the tools and knowledge they needed to lead their teams effectively without getting frustrated. Many were beginning to question whether they were cut out for management.

I wanted to help as many managers as possible ease the frustration of leading in today's constantly changing workplace. To do so, I created my flagship program, Managing Made Easy™, a six-module cohort-based group program that equips managers with the core management tools they need to lead people.

A key factor that adds to the frustration many managers are facing comes from the fact that the companies they are working for are operating from antiquated knowledge and management practices adopted from a different time. Certain management behaviors still being encouraged today are outdated and not as healthy or positive as they appear.

Without realizing it, companies can support the wrong behavior in their managers without considering the impact of these negative practices. Some examples of these outdated leadership practices that send the wrong messages to employees include the "feedback sandwich," annual performance reviews, and statements like "Don't bring me problems, bring me solutions."

I will address outdated management habits I notice companies still using in this book as well. Because there is no point in attempting to adopt new practices until you realize why the ones you currently use are ineffective.

My hope for all the busy managers, executives, and business owners reading this book is that it will help you find a deeper understanding of why you are experiencing frustration in your role. This understanding will come with some uncomfortable realizations, including that your employees are not always the problem.

You are also partly responsible for the performance of your team. This brings me to the first tool every manager must have in their toolbox—the willingness and awareness to question their own thoughts, beliefs, and expectations about being a manager.

EVALUATING YOUR THOUGHTS AND BELIEFS—*WHAT IF I DON'T WANT TO MANAGE, I WANT TO LEAD?*

The way leadership and management are portrayed contributes to some of the frustration managers are experiencing today. On a routine visit to my dentist's office for a cleaning, the dental hygienist asked about my work. Once again, I listened to a former frustrated manager tell me their story about how they hated the managing aspects of their role but loved the leadership aspects. The hygienist had his hands in my mouth, so I couldn't explain that the difference between management and leadership is your perception about the work you are doing.

Henry Mintzberg captures the relationship between leadership and management perfectly. Mintzberg is a Canadian academic and author on business and management and is currently the Cleghorn Professor of Management Studies at the Desautels Faculty of Management of McGill University in Montreal, Quebec. "Managers who don't lead are quite discouraging," Mintzberg observes, "but leaders who don't manage don't know what's going on. It's a phony separation that people are making between the two."

Mintzberg also describes a clear approach to developing management and leadership capabilities:

- Managers and leaders cannot be created in the classroom.
- Managing is learned on the job, strengthened by varied work experiences.
- Development programs help managers make meaning of their experiences.
- Learning must be transferred back to the workplace if it is to have impact.
- The above needs to be organized, based on the nature of managing.

My experience and understanding of leadership and management is that you can't have one without the other. I explain management and leadership as "management is what you are doing" and leadership is "who you are being." A modern manager strikes the balance of leading and managing to bring out the best in others while moving goals forward.

In any given activity or conversation, a manager can leverage the skills of a manager and the behaviors of a leader. When you are delegating a task to an employee, you are executing a key management function. As you delegate, you can ask the employee about their ideas of what success looks like as they complete this task, and then you are leading as you help the employee harness a vision.

I understand the frustration coming from my dental hygienist that day. He explained that he used to feel like he was babysitting an employee who was often late for work. The fact that he referred to his role as "babysitting" confirms that he did not have the right mindset about his role. Yes, if you decide that reminding an employee of what time work begins is all you are responsible for, you are in fact a glorified babysitter. If you decide to approach the problem of a consistently late employee by getting curious about what might be going on with the employee and have an open conversation with them, then you are taking a people-first, human approach to your management role. The choice is yours. One approach will result in frustration. Another will result in the situation likely being resolved once and for all and a sense of satisfaction that you supported your team member.

Operating from a management belief system that is not helpful for leading a team will increase frustrations. Remember, what you believe, you attract. When you go to work each day, you have two choices. You can tell yourself that today is another opportunity to work with your team in a way that will bring out the best in each other, *or* you can allow limiting thoughts and beliefs to drive unrealistic expectations related to what it takes to lead a team effectively and joyfully.

Our thoughts and beliefs have tremendous power over our satisfaction and success in our lives and careers. Do you believe you can be a good manager? Do you like people? Do you believe in people? Do you want them to succeed? Once you have considered how your thoughts, beliefs, and expectations affect your ability to lead, it's time to move on to the five core frustrations of being a manager today.

In my ten years of leadership coaching, I have heard it all regarding the various thoughts and beliefs many managers and business owners have about management. I have heard people say things like "I don't have time to babysit a group of employees." Or "I shouldn't have to stay on top of people to get things done." And, my favorite, "If it weren't for the HR part, running a business would be easy." If you hear yourself saying something similar, it is time for your own mindset shift. I have also heard managers say they are considering going back to being an individual performer because they are not sure being in a management role is worth it.

The journey to becoming a modern manager who inspires performance, as opposed to one who has to be a driver of performance, requires as much unlearning and mindset shifts as learning new technical skills and tools. The day-to-day work of a manager is rarely glamorous. It consists of delegating, feedback conversations, all the meetings, and so many other tasks. And since these unsexy tasks are not represented on inspirational social feeds, I want you to know that I see you and know how hard you are working to be a great manager for your team!

This is why I wrote this book and created my programs. I want managers to have the tools they need to do their jobs so they can get past the initial frustration that can come with leading a team and tap into the joy of developing others and watching them succeed.

Early in my career I found myself working with a true people-first leader, a *modern manager*. It has been over fifteen years since I spoke with this person, but I still remember how I felt in their presence. I had just been promoted to my first team-leader role. I was working on an interdepartmental project, and I was eager to make a good impression. I had already run into an issue with a member of the team from another department, and I didn't know how to handle it. The project came to a screeching halt, and I was avoiding my own manager because I did not want to admit I didn't know how to handle the situation. The director from the other department working on the project approached me one day to ask for an update. She came to me and sat in my office. She didn't make me go to her. She asked how her team members were doing on the project before asking how the project itself was doing. She probably sensed that things weren't going well, or she knew her team members well enough to know that an inexperienced manager might struggle when working with them. I began confessing that I didn't know how to handle one team member and didn't know how to move past the issue. What happened next blew my mind. The director was compassionate and understanding. She didn't blame anyone. She gave me some guidance and instruction on what to do when work styles and personalities clash on a project and told me she would speak with her team members. I exhaled so loudly I am sure the entire department heard. What made the biggest difference was that she came to me when she sensed something was wrong. She didn't wait for me to come to her.

Employees today want a manager who cares about them and will support them through their challenges as that director did for me. A modern manager is not a parent, friend, or counselor. They do, however, coach and empower team members. A modern manager has the skill to ensure smooth workflow, clearly communicates priorities and expectations, and supports the success of their team members. When a modern manager must navigate performance issues, they do so from a mindset of curiosity and with empathy. Skills and attributes such as adaptability, problem-solving, and critical thinking are essential for a modern manager to be able to respond to changing dynamics while remaining resilient. And, of course, they are aware of and manage the frustrations that come with being a modern people manager so they can lead effectively.

I've written this book to reduce the learning curve and the stress level for managers of all levels to ease their pain and help them find joy in leading others. I want to ensure no manager questions whether it is worth it to be in their role. Ready? Let's get started.

CHAPTER 1

How Did We Get Here?

Despite leveraging technology to improve how we work, we still base much of our lives on an outdated twentieth-century model incompatible with the performance and outcomes companies expect today. This mismatch is the source of our current state of affairs and is at the heart of a great deal of frustration between employees, managers, executives, and company owners. It can also be a source of frustration for customers, which has impacts on the bottom line.

Our school systems are still based on that same outmoded factory model. Young people graduate and go on to get jobs in a corporate system still tied to the forty-hour workweek. Productivity is measured by hours worked, not by the quality of the outcome produced. Author and speaker Seth Godin said it best: "Every year, we churn out millions of workers who are trained to do 1925-style labor."

In other words, whereas technology has completely transformed how we *do* our work, *how* we work has not changed much. The twentieth-century model was indeed effective for producing a set number of "widgets" each day. It does not, however, make sense for today's knowledge or digital workers, who often produce their best work—and derive much of their sense of fulfillment and satisfaction—when provided with greater autonomy and greater latitude as to how and when they work. Yet too many companies stick to the old ways and still expect the same level of productivity, commitment, and innovation, a level achievable only when team members can reach a state of flow. And flow is difficult, if not impossible, to reach consistently in today's fast-paced and fast-growth organizations, where days are full of interruptions and aimless meetings and are poorly structured for high-quality output.

Where does this get us? To a place where unhappy, exhausted employees and managers answer to executives or business owners who don't understand "why no one wants to work anymore."

Employees do want to work, and they have been aiming for greater autonomy for years. Nowhere is this clearer than with the desire for remote-work options, an issue on which it took a global pandemic for many companies to bend. Companies have a bad habit of refusing employees' requests unless absolutely required to grant them in any case, but with COVID's onset, they knew they couldn't stay in business without compromise. Teams proved then that they could, in fact, be productive from home—more productive, even. Now, job seekers routinely seek out a remote-work option first. With the height of the pandemic behind us, companies are slipping back into old ways: many look for any excuse to justify bringing employees back into the office. "Remote work is not conducive to our culture of collaboration," they often insist. Few employees buy that line, but they comply because they need jobs, and their managers are left to deal with subtle grievances and a trend toward disengagement.

It likely comes as no surprise when we consider the demands on managers today that many, especially middle managers, are experiencing higher rates of burnout than ever. Research from Columbia University in 2015 found 18 percent of middle managers reported symptoms of depression, compared to 12 percent for blue-collar workers and 11 percent for owners and executives.[3] Millennial managers are far more likely than managers of any other generation to report burnout.[4] The glorification of overwork combined with the demands of caring for children and parents have contributed to the strain.

CHANGING NEEDS AND EXPECTATIONS

Technology, pandemics—whatever the case, workplaces naturally evolve. And employees' expectations and needs evolve right alongside. Tools like LinkedIn and Glassdoor, for instance, have empowered us to research a company's culture before even applying. Word gets out fast in our connected world, and if a company has garnered a reputation as a bad place to work, recruitment can be a challenge.

What does this mean for today's managers, who too often find themselves unsupported and ill-equipped to ride the curve of change? It means navigating competing and sometimes unrealistic expectations from both employees and executives. Today's manager is trying on the one hand to lead in an environment that values fast growth and questionable measures of productivity over quality, while on the other dealing with increasing employee expectations and demands. Leading a team is not straightforward. A manager is not someone who simply coordinates work and ensures results are met. The modern manager is expected to support the professional growth of their employees, care about their well-being, act as a coach and mentor, delegate, and get results, all while doing their own work and taking care of their career.

An example of a major workplace dynamic managers have been tasked with is supporting the mental health of their employees. Psychological safety and well-being are now considered an integral aspect of a company's overall approach to health and safety. I fully support integrating psychological safety into the overall health and safety of employees, *and* managers need significant training and support to understand how to navigate conversations with employees about their mental health.[5] In the past ten years, my team and I have experienced an increase in the number of managers expressing frustration that employees are coming to them and disclosing their mental health issues. It is a welcome change to remove the stigma from mental health conversations. With that said, managers are not counselors, and most of them have not received training in mental health first aid or training on how to respond to this type of disclosure from an employee. Expecting managers to know how to respond appropriately to an employee's mental health disclosure without proper training is unrealistic and could traumatize the manager and the employee. Many managers are experiencing their own mental health challenges, and it can be a struggle to help others in an area where you are also struggling.[6]

THE PERFECT STORM FOR MANAGERS

An outdated twentieth-century model, evolving expectations and demands, bad managerial advice that won't die, poor leadership development strategies—altogether it's a perfect storm of frustrations for those who lead.

Further, managers are no longer expected merely to plan and organize work. They are expected to be people leaders, with exceptional communication skills, who can also support the growing needs of their employees, including providing mental health support. Easy, right? I don't believe that leading a team must be that hard. But I do know that without the right tools, it will be much harder than it needs to be. Now more than ever, managers need a skill set with the knowledge, tools, and techniques that will help them understand how to inspire performance from employees.

With this perfect storm that largely seems out of the hands of managers, you might be wondering why you should bother making improvements to your managerial approach. The simple answer is we must be the change we want to see. Even if your current workplace does not have the type of culture that inspires the best from its workforce, you can still create a culture on your team that is conducive to everyone doing their best work. A strong team performing at its best means less stress and better outcomes for everybody. We would also begin to see a positive exponential effect in our workplaces if all new managers were properly equipped for their role and carried those skills with them as they forged ahead in their careers. Change must start somewhere, and the bottom-up effort will eventually translate into an effort led from the top once those well-trained first-time managers become seasoned executives.

I have witnessed the impact firsthand when one frustrated manager attends a webinar of mine, signs up for my program, and returns to work to share their learnings with their colleagues. Smart companies act quickly to sign up the remainder of their managers so everyone has the same training. The result is improved manager experience, which reduces management turnover, increases employee engagement overall, and makes it easier to attract more talent. Each manager who applies the strategies and tools learned in this book contributes to a broader initiative aimed at reshaping leadership and organizational norms to align with contemporary demands and realities.

PROMOTING STAR TECHNICAL EMPLOYEES TO MANAGEMENT

The way companies select a manager when promoting internally has also not changed. Companies are still promoting a star team player to lead that team on the assumption that a strong technical employee will surely be a good leader of that team. And in many cases, not providing them with any new-manager training. As new managers become aware of the challenge of leading others, they begin to question whether they are "cut out for management" before they have been given any tools for their new role. It's like asking someone to be a carpenter and only giving them a screwdriver in their toolbox.

There was a time when consultants like me would shout, "STOP DOING THIS!" from the rooftops. I don't speak for all consultants, but I can tell you that I surrendered to this battle a long time ago. I do not waste my time arguing with reality. Today, I advise companies on how to effectively select and develop emerging leaders within their organization based on a defined set of leadership competencies. Your organization can do this work internally if it has the resources, or you can work with a leadership consultant like me.

Does Your Company Struggle to Promote from Within?

What is the typical reaction at your company when employees are asked if they want to step up to a management role? Is it less than enthusiastic, as in: "I don't need the headache!" or "It's not worth it"?

Leadership succession affects all aspects of business, from productivity to employee engagement. If employees are not eager to take on a leadership role, it could be a sign that new managers feel there is not enough support to succeed in management. Employees may have witnessed the struggles their own or other managers have experienced when navigating their own workload alongside a supervisory function.

If your organization struggles to promote from

within, do not wait until an employee is officially in the role to start their leadership development. Demonstrate that you support potential and emerging leaders by providing training in areas such as communication skills, emotional intelligence, and conflict management.

A former coaching client who I consider to be a high-performing employee left her employer when she was recruited by another tech company and offered a higher salary. After experiencing difficulties with her new manager, who didn't know how to support her and remove the obstacles preventing her from doing her best work, she left the company and returned to her former employer. An ineffective manager can result in the loss of a good employee, which her new employer learned the hard way. Her old employer, however, does invest in leadership development for all their managers and will always be a more attractive option for talented people who do not tolerate ineffective leadership.

Companies must take time to consider what makes a good leader at their company and start noticing who already possesses some of the behaviors and habits of a good leader. An employee's reaction to taking on more responsibility will tell you everything you need to know about the perceived level of support for new managers at your company.

MULTIGENERATIONAL WORKPLACES

Workplaces can have up to five generations, and therefore it is not unusual for a manager to have a direct report who is older than them. In fact, it's one of the most common scenarios brought to me by first-time managers because there is typically someone on their team who is older and has more experience. And sometimes the entire team is older and more experienced.

According to the Pew Research Center,[7] there are about forty million employees from the baby boom generation and about fifty-five million employees from the millennial generation in today's workforce. This data is taken from the entire US workforce, but what this means is that every fourth employee in the workforce is a baby boomer, while every third is from a younger generation. As a result, there will be a lot of instances when the manager is from a different generation than their team members, and in many cases, the manager is from a younger generation.

I will not be addressing generational differences and how to lead each generation. Generational characterizations can be problematic and cause greater division. People are more than the generation they are born into, and many of the labels and stereotypes given to each generation have been exacerbated by the media. I encourage managers to get to know each team member individually to uncover their own unique work styles and motivations. Being a manager to employees who are older than you can, however, provide another layer of complexity and stress for the manager. I have coached many managers on how to overcome the awkwardness that comes with asking questions like "Who am I to be leading someone who is older and therefore has more experience than me?"

BAD ADVICE AND LEADERSHIP ACCORDING TO SOCIAL MEDIA

There is no shortage of advice on how to manage and lead a team. Outdated advice can be a catalyst for the frustrations of today's manager. Ask five managers, executives, or business owners how to handle a "people problem" at work and you will get five different approaches. Social media platforms are a constant stream of vague platitudes on leadership, out-of-context blanket advice, and inspirational quotes from Richard Branson and other celebrity-type CEOs. The plethora of platitudinal leadership posts on TikTok, Instagram, and LinkedIn also tend to get the most shares and likes. The applause for vague and obvious posts such as "Choose the right team and trust them to deliver" is disheartening. The conflicting tips and approaches on how to lead in a modern-day workplace can make a manager's head spin.

Some of the worst advice and strategies still offered up to first-time managers today include the following:

1. On your first day as a manager, pick a fight with someone and win.
2. Use the feedback sandwich when delivering criticism. (More on this in chapter 4.)
3. Hire smart people and get out of their way.
4. Hire slow and fire fast.

Most of this advice and strategy came out of the 1980s to

early 2000s or from poorly thought-out social media posts that too often romanticize *leadership* while making *management* a dirty word. Some advice is vague and so lacking in context that if a manager were to take it at face value, they could be setting themselves and their team up for failure. For instance, hopefully you are hiring smart people to be on your team. But the advice about "people don't need to be managed" and "getting out of their way" lacks nuance. Nor is it exactly true. Even smart employees require support and need to be informed on expectations and priorities.

What would happen in any company if every manager bought into the social media definition of leadership and decided to walk around acting like a visionary? Lots of dreamers, not enough doers. When it comes to work, we would all be better served if we stopped looking at "management" as the ugly stepchild it has been made out to be and instead embrace it for what it is—a necessary role in every company that requires a specific skill set and tools to be done well. The information that does not get included with the romanticized posts about leadership is that for every Jobs and Branson there was a crackerjack COO standing next to them who was executing everything. In other words, a good manager.

The real problem with vague platitudes on social media and outdated advice from the 1990s is that they oversimplify what it takes to be an effective team leader today. Add this to an atmosphere where most seem to be looking for a shortcut to solve their problems and you have a real issue.

If you have read these posts and wonder why leading a team doesn't feel like this for you, it's because it is rarely that simple. If your vision of leadership comes from these types of vague platitudes yet it doesn't feel or look like this when you lead your team, you create *dissonance*. In other words, you will have tension between your vision for you and your team and your day-to-day reality of being a manager.

EXPECTATION MANAGEMENT

We create our own frustrations when we have unrealistic expectations of how it will be to lead a team. Blaming employees for our frustrations and labeling them as underperformers is unjust when we didn't anticipate the realistic time required for new hires to become fully onboarded and share our workload. When I explain a realistic timeline for onboarding a new employee to managers, the common reaction is "I think I've been expecting too much." New managers are especially prone to frustration and disappointment when they don't know what to expect in their new role.

The minute I realized I was pregnant with my son, in 2009, I picked up a copy of *What to Expect When You're Expecting*, one of the most popular pregnancy books on the market. And if you are a parent, you know that no matter how many pregnancy books you read, you are rarely prepared for what actually happens when you bring baby home.

The same goes for new managers: a lot of ambitious employees reach out to me to ask if there is anything they can read to prepare themselves for their first management role. I applaud their eagerness to learn and desire to get it right. I always share a list of the most useful books and articles on management and leadership. And I remind managers that management is typically much harder in practice than even the best leadership books can describe, just as parenting is harder than any reading material makes it out to be.

We still expect managers to look and act in a certain way. I received a call once from a frustrated thirtysomething small-business manager proclaiming, "I am the youngest person in the company, so why am I the one leading everything?" He was consistently actioning ideas and taking initiative to grow the business, yet he thought the owners and managers "should" be telling him what to do.

We need to manage our own expectations and ideas about what leadership looks like. Management doesn't have an age requirement anymore, for instance. You can be a leader at any age. There was a time when managers were typically the oldest person or the most experienced person on the team—yet another outdated perception left over from the industrial age. Old-school ideas of leadership based on title and authority are often at the source of frustration for many employees and managers.

UNLEARNING BAD ADVICE AND LETTING GO OF OLD HABITS

You may have already reflected on some of your own management missteps since stepping into your first management role. Those mistakes may have come from bad management advice still circulating in the halls of corporate and university textbooks or from habits you formed out of the need to cope because you didn't receive any training in how to be a good manager. Forgive yourself for what you didn't know and let go of those mistakes. Make room in your mind and your identity to become a new kind of manager—a people-first manager who communicates with exceptional clarity, delegates with ease, provides high-quality feedback, and responds to the needs of each employee to bring out their individual greatness.

Unlearning is a critical part of learning. I encourage you to journal on some of the advice you've received in the past. Does it sound like it aligns with the type of manager you want to be and the type of manager your employees need you to be? What has worked for you and your team in the past, and what has not worked? Assemble your own leadership tool kit and set the course for how you want to show up each day for your team. You can build the skills you need by naming, identifying, and analyzing the core frustrations you face as manager every day—starting with micromanagement.

CHAPTER 2

Frustration #1—Micromanagement Misunderstanding: Am I Managing Too Much or Too Little?

Seventeen years ago, I was a frustrated employee trying to figure out how to deal with a manager who, to put it mildly, was very hands-on. My morale and confidence were fading fast under her thumb. As I cc'd her on yet another email, I vowed that I would never micromanage my team should I ever become a manager.

My time did come. Faster than I'd anticipated. I was working for that same manager when she informed me one of my project proposals was approved and I could go ahead and build my project team. I was over the moon. Finally, the chance to prove myself and grow my career.

I spent two months in the field setting up the project, then hiring and onboarding the right people to execute the work. I trained them, gave them the resources they needed to do the work, and then returned to my office to continue working on the day-to-day aspects of my role. I had other projects that needed my attention.

Two months after the project began, I set up a check-in meeting with the team. I was expecting a debrief and plenty of success stories, but instead I listened to two hours of problems and issues from upset team members. I was quickly filled with frustration. I asked them why they didn't reach out to let me know about their issues and was shocked when they said, "We got the impression you didn't want updates from us. You disappeared after the project launch, and we didn't want to bother you."

My frustration quickly turned to embarrassment. How could this have gone so wrong? Didn't they see I was giving them the autonomy that I craved but didn't get from my manager?

When I returned to my office, I asked a colleague to go for a walk at lunch so I could vent about the situation with her.

> **Corina:** Sarah, I'm really struggling with my new team. I vowed I would never micromanage like my manager. But when I gave them space to do their work, they just got bogged down in obstacles and didn't do anything to

move forward. I shouldn't have to micromanage them, right? They should know what to do.

Sarah: I understand your frustration. It's not uncommon for new managers to feel this way. Tell me more about the situation.

Corina: Well, it's just that I thought hiring the right people would make my job easier. I onboarded and trained them, so I thought they could run with it after that. They do have a lot of experience. But should I have watched over their shoulders more closely?

Sarah: It's natural to expect team members to excel, especially when they've been carefully selected for the role. But remember, management is a skill, just like any other. Sometimes, it's not about finding fault with the team, but rather understanding how you can empower them to perform better.

Corina: But how can I empower them? Shouldn't they take responsibility for their own work?

Sarah: Absolutely, they should. But as a manager, it's your role to provide the necessary support, guidance, and feedback. Think of it this way—your team is like a ship sailing toward a destination, and you're the captain. While you want your crew to be skilled and motivated, you also need to chart the course, steer the ship, and adjust sails when needed.

Corina: I see your point, but what is the

point of hiring a team if I must constantly check in and guide them?

Sarah: Because it's about fostering a culture of accountability and continuous improvement. Part of your role as their team leader is striking the right balance between trusting your team and providing support. Have you suggested any one-on-one meetings or regular team check-ins with the team to get updates and find out if they are experiencing obstacles?

Corina: I did suggest monthly check-ins, but I think I will increase the frequency to weekly check-ins until we iron out the wrinkles in this project. Then we can probably cut back to biweekly.

Sarah: That's a great idea. Remember, check-ins should provide a safe space to address concerns and for dealing with challenges they encounter. One-on-ones can be used for giving specific feedback without the pressure of a group setting.

Corina: This conversation has been helpful. I guess in my desire to *not* micromanage, I went too far and didn't provide enough guidance and support. I need to step up as a manager and provide the support my team needs.

Sarah: You are not alone. A lot of first-time managers who understand the negative impact of micromanaging go too far in the other direction. Remember, initiating regular check-ins is not micromanaging, it's just *managing*.

WHAT IS THE REAL PROBLEM, AND WHY IS THIS FRUSTRATING?

I will never forget that conversation with my colleague. I was embarrassed by my results and my approach to leading a team. Now that I have trained and coached hundreds of managers through my business, I realize that for many first-time managers, being labeled a micromanager by their team is considered a fate worse than death. First-time managers today are so afraid of being labeled a micromanager that, in many cases, they are not managing enough.

Micromanaging has been around long enough to garner a reputation as negative and soul crushing for an employee. We have all heard the stories about the manager who watches over their employee's shoulder and restricts their efforts.

In an article written for *Public Personnel Management*, Richard D. White, author and Marjory B. Ourso Excellence in Teaching Professor of Public Administration at Louisiana State University, states that "Micromanagement has been practiced and recognized well before we labeled it as an organizational pathology."[8] In 1946, Peter Drucker called for a "democracy of management" whereby organizations need to decentralize and delegate more decision-making authority to employees. Many employees today are still asking for more decision-making authority in how and when they do their work. White also states, "While micromanagement has always disrupted organizational life, it only recently has entered the workplace vocabulary, with the first mention of the term appearing in 1975 in an article in the *Economist*."

Given the lengthy history of micromanagement in the workplace and the many horror stories circulating about "horrible bosses," it is to be expected that managers today would rather risk not managing enough than ever managing too much. In fact, one of the most common questions I get from first-time managers is "How can I keep my team and the work on track *without* being a micromanager?" The answer does not lie in taking a hands-off approach, as I did in my story, and risk leaving your "ship without a captain."

This micromanagement misunderstanding will cause first-time managers a great deal of frustration because they think they are doing the right thing (just like I did) by giving team members space to do their job. Team members, on the other hand, may need more training, direction, guidance, and accountability to complete the work to the timeline and standard. It is time to address the confusion around micromanagement and alleviate the worry for managers.

WHAT ARE MICRO- AND MACROMANAGEMENT?

When we hear the term *micromanagement*, images of controlling bosses breathing down our necks likely come to mind and send a chill down our spines. No one wants to earn that title. And because of the negative publicity of this management style, managers tend to think that any amount of oversight of team members means they are micromanaging.

At its worst, micromanaging is constantly telling an employee *how* to do their job, often down to the smallest detail, even when they are more than capable of doing it without your close supervision. There is also often a lot of controlling behavior (e.g., telling an employee to "cc me on everything"). It is restricting autonomy and ensuring you are in the know on every detail of your employee's work. Micromanaging is also taking back the work and doing it yourself because you don't think anyone can do it as good as you. Micromanaging is making employees physically come back into the office because if you can't see them working, you don't trust that they are working.

Micromanagers also tend to refuse to pass on skills or knowledge necessary for an employee to do their job well, something which often stems from a fear of being replaced or made obsolete. After all, if someone else knows how to do it, why would they need you?

Obviously, this type of behavior crushes morale. But because I leave nothing to guesswork, let's also talk about what is not micromanaging.

Conducting regular check-ins with team members and asking for updates on deliverables—these are not signs of micromanaging. They are normal functions of management. Giving an employee feedback on their performance is also part of the role. Setting expectations and establishing milestones are normal and expected practices in management and are not considered micromanagement. These activities are just *managing*.

Getting clear on the line between micromanaging and simply managing can alleviate the concern that you are watching over employees too closely.

But here's the other side of my experience in my career before I left to start my own business. While I had one severe micromanager, I had two macromanagers. *Macromanagement* can be just as bad as micromanagement (maybe worse). Also known as an *absentee manager,* a macromanager can leave a team feeling like a crew without a captain and—speaking from personal experience—can be just as challenging for team members as micromanagement.

Everything has pros and cons. Micro- and macromanagement can have a negative impact, but there is also a time to manage more closely and a time to step back and give an employee space. Let's clarify the confusion around these two management styles and the consequences of not understanding how to strike a management balance between overmanaging and undermanaging.

Let's define *macromanagement* since macromanagement is rarely discussed in the leadership sphere and is more prevalent these days than micromanagement. Macromanagement is a hands-off approach to leading a team. It is a management style where the manager provides high-level detail about the work to a team but is not involved in the day-to-day aspect. Employees have a high level of autonomy over their work.

Sounds great, right? Except macromanagement can also go too far and leave team members without support and guidance. Macromanagement at its worst is absentee management, which is what I did when I set up a project team and then disappeared for two months and thought I was crushing my new role as team leader.

Macromanagement can also come from an avoidant manager. Many managers decide they don't want to get involved in certain aspects of the people side of management, especially conflicts or employee disputes. Allowing negativity or conflict to go unaddressed and unresolved on a team can often lead to long-term team dysfunction.

Another example of extreme macromanagement is when the manager or business owner is not even in the building. A friend and colleague accepted a role as director of a government department. She was excited about the job, so when we had a chance to catch up, I asked her how it was going. She immediately expressed her disappointment that her executive director was only two years away from retirement and had filled her calendar with unused vacation time and conferences. Her ED was literally out of the office, leaving my friend to muddle through her new role. She didn't realize this was the situation when she accepted the job. She dealt with it by asking for support from a longtime director in an adjacent department until a new executive director was hired.

There is a lot of space in between micro- and macromanagement where a good manager can evaluate the needs of each direct report to understand how much support the employee will need from them. The Manager's Scale is a tool I developed to help managers navigate this space, to gauge when they will have to manage more and when they can manage less. In other words, it takes the guesswork out of managing.

I developed this tool to provide clarity on what micro- and macromanagement really mean and what is required from a manager to develop an employee to get the best performance possible from them. For any manager who has ever worried that they are micromanaging, this tool will help alleviate their concerns and provide answers if managers are not getting what they need from their team members.

FINDING A MANAGEMENT BALANCE: THE MANAGER'S SCALE

Managers fear the micromanager label for three reasons. The first is because they suffered under the "rule" of a micromanager and don't want to make the same mistake, so they go too far in the other direction. Second, an employee who doesn't want to be managed at all once accused them of micromanaging. Third, the manager thinks that checking in for an update with an employee means they are doing something wrong. A good employee is proactive in providing updates on their progress to their manager, but requesting an update is not necessarily indicative of micromanaging.

Whatever the source of the fear, learning how to find a balance between not managing too much or too little will ensure you provide the right level of support to an employee so you can both excel. Managers at all stages of their leadership journey can learn from my mistakes and find the right balance where you manage your team just enough.

Striking this balance of not managing too much or too little with each employee on your team requires two things: fully understanding the role of a manager, and getting to know your employee and their capabilities.

There will be a time when you must spend more time on the micro side of the scale with an employee to train them and provide them with enough direction to learn their role. If an employee is new to the team or the task they have been assigned, for example, you will need to check in more often. Once that employee has achieved competence in the task and their role, you can move further down the scale, where you can be a facilitator and a partner in their success by involving the employee in more discussions about team goals. Eventually, when an employee is fully competent and confident in their role, you can be the coach and empower the employee to solve their own problems.

Once you have leveraged onboarding, training, and coaching to develop an employee to the point where they are fully competent and trustworthy, you can move toward the other end of the scale, toward macromanagement. Managers earn the right to macromanage by taking all necessary steps to develop and support their employees.

Between the scale's extreme ends of micro- and macromanagement are opportunities where you will be required to train, teach, onboard, direct, delegate, partner with, facilitate, empower, coach, and collaborate.

The Manager's Scale will help you to self-assess your current management style (and self-correct if needed) and determine the needs of your employees and to understand how much oversight and support teams need from you. You can assess, not guess, how closely you have been managing and recognize when you are approaching the danger zone of managing too much or too little and quickly self-correct.

THE MANAGER'S SCALE

Command & Control Doing/Fixing	Teaching/ Training Onboarding Directing	Partnering Facilitating Collaborating	Coaching Empowering Delegating	Absentee Avoiding/ Abdicating

MICROMANAGEMENT ←————— ▲ —————→ MACROMANAGEMENT

You should ensure you stay away from the areas on each end of the scale, also known as the "danger zones" of management. The danger zone of micromanagement is controlling behavior, and the danger zone of macromanagement is absentee or avoidant behavior. As you can see from the scale, there is plenty of space in the middle for positive management approaches you can use based on the amount of support and oversight required to set an employee up for success.

An employee may be new to your team but deeply experienced with a similar type of work. In this situation, the employee requires onboarding to the company and the team to feel welcomed but may not need as much oversight on the technical aspects of their role. On the other hand, a new graduate will need both onboarding into the company and the team as well as training for their role, and it may take longer before you feel comfortable moving further along the scale toward the macro side.

My husband, for instance, accepted a role with a new organization three years after graduation. He was immediately assigned a mentor whose job was to onboard him into the department and his role. What should have been an exciting experience quickly turned to frustration. My husband was skilled and confident at the technical aspects of his job. What he needed was organizational onboarding, including information on operational norms and processes. His mentor failed to recognize what he needed to successfully onboard and treated him like a new grad by attempting to train him on the technical aspects of this role.

My husband raised his concerns with the department head and received a response of "We are aware of the issues with this particular mentor." The department knew about the issue and opted to ignore it. He managed to get through his four-week orientation (which was only scheduled for two weeks) when he quietly asked his supervisor to pair him with a different mentor.

Had his mentor and organization had a tool like the Manager's Scale, this situation could have been avoided.

Michelle is a dedicated HR manager who completed my group program. She had a team of HR assistants, two of whom she considered competent, resourceful high performers who would come to her when they ran into any issues. They proactively updated her on progress; she didn't need to ask. Michelle could macromanage these two, in other words. These two HR assistants—ideal employees for any manager—had earned her trust through their performance and initiative. Michelle could choose a management style on the macro end such as coaching, delegating, and empowering for these two employees. If Michelle were to assign a new project to one of them for which they had no experience, she would need to choose a management style closer to the micro end of the scale, such as training or partnering with the employee until they are feeling confident with the new work.

A third assistant on Michelle's team was newer to the organization and her role. She was less confident in her own abilities and hadn't yet established effective performance habits. Using the Manager's Scale, Michelle assessed how closely she would need to work with this HR assistant and how much support she would need to provide to help her build her own competence and confidence. Michelle knew she needed to set clear expectations and transparent milestones, and the new assistant's level of responsibility would need to increase gradually. As performance improved, Michelle could reduce oversight and move toward the macro side of the scale.

A key underlying reason for the frustration of a manager's experience is they have told themselves a story that "they shouldn't have to micromanage or babysit" an employee. Providing support by way of onboarding, training, setting clear expectations, and answering questions for an employee is not micromanaging. It is just managing. And once a manager has invested their time and belief into an employee's competence and confidence, that manager has earned the right to macromanage and reap the benefits of an engaged high performer.

If you worry whether you are in the danger zones of managing too closely or not enough, the best approach is the simplest one: ask your team members! Don't guess whether they are getting the right level of support from you. "Is my hovering driving you crazy?" "Are you frustrated and in need of guidance?" Lean into this approach and you won't have to guess how much guidance and support each team member needs from you.

It's not enough to focus on *not* micromanaging your employees to be an effective manager. A modern manager must know how to partner and collaborate with their teams to achieve success and bring out the best in everyone. If you are willing to commit to a process of training your new employee, delegating, reviewing their work, providing constructive feedback, and letting them try again, eventually you will have a great employee who consistently produces high-quality work. This is the point where you can switch from managing to leading the employee, and you will finally start to feel the relief of having a competent, engaged employee on your team.

BECOMING A RESPONSIVE MANAGER

Remember my story from the beginning of this chapter? I was so focused on the type of manager I didn't want to be, I went too far in the other direction. Responsive people management means meeting employees where they are. You communicate and engage with your team in a way that is responsive to their needs. You can only do that when you are not creating an expectation for how you think an employee "should" perform or how quickly they should learn.

I don't think anyone accepts a promotion to their first management role thinking *I can't wait to stay on top of my team to make sure the work gets done.* Yet most managers I meet think that is what they must do to keep work moving forward, and at the same time, they are terrified of being a micromanager. This dissonance will undoubtably cause a lot of frustration for any manager. You must also remember that your employees want you to lead. No employee ever walked into work on a Monday saying, "I can't wait to sit at my desk all day and wonder what the priorities are." Employees want to know what is expected of them, and no one will ever thrive if they have confusion about their role. Employees want to know what they are working toward. So do not confuse delegating, setting expectations, and giving feedback with micromanaging. It is just managing.

Your employees are happier when they know and

understand what is expected of them and where they stand with their performance. *Embrace* your leadership role as an opportunity to make your employees' lives better!

The Manager's Scale will help you take a *responsive* approach to leading your team so you never *over-* or *undermanage*. Remember, each employee on a team will need something different from you. In a hybrid or remote-work environment, understanding how to be a responsive manager is even more important. So don't choose a management style based on your previous experience with a manager. Take time to get to know each of your team members and understand that the same management style will not work for everyone.

A responsive manager is present, supportive, and willing to have those crucial conversations that will propel the team forward. When you find your place on the Manager's Scale that is required for the employee, you are more likely able to inspire results from your team members. When you base your management style off outdated notions of what it means to be a good manager, you are likely going to end up having to be a *driver* of results.

I remember the first day of my last job. My new director showed me to my office, gave me a tour of the building, introduced me to a handful of people, and then I didn't see her again for two weeks. Most of us have experienced working for a bad manager, and that experience can shape who we become as leaders in both positive and negative ways. If you have had a negative experience with your own manager, you can reflect on that experience and use it to your advantage. But remember that every employee is different and will likely need something different from you as their manager. Being a responsive manager is more likely to set you up for success rather than deciding to take the opposite approach of your last manager. Don't let your hyperawareness about the negative impact of micromanagement get in the way of cultivating effective management habits with your team. If you focus on becoming the kind of manager your employees need you to be, you will have an engaged, productive team.

Achieving balance as a manager is also about resilience and career longevity, not just what your employees need. Many of the managers who reach out to me for help are feeling worn out and defeated. They are not sure they even want to be a manager anymore and are reminiscing about life as an employee, when they didn't have the responsibility of someone else's performance on their plate. I don't believe that being a manager has to be hard. But I do know that frustration and exhaustion will set in quickly for new managers if they are missing the tools they need to lead effectively and bring out the best in their team.

Now that you understand what micromanaging really is and what it is not, it's time to look at how you delegate. There is almost as much confusion around delegating as there is about micromanagement, so clarity in this area will alleviate the second-greatest cause of a manager's frustration.

END-OF-CHAPTER REFLECTION, EXERCISES, AND TOOLS:

1. Reflect on your experience with past managers who were not the leader you needed them to be at the time. Appreciate the wisdom you gained from learning how *not* to lead. Then, channel some

empathy for them because they likely thought what they were doing was what was needed at that time.
2. Journal on how you want to engage with your team on a daily and weekly basis.
3. Consider what type of support and leadership your team members need from you right now to become the best version of themselves. Not sure? Just ask them!

> Here are some questions you can ask your team members in your next 1:1 meeting:
>
> - Am I giving you too much detail or not enough detail when I delegate?
> - Are we meeting often enough for you to feel supported?
> - What is getting in the way of you doing your job?
> - What kind of support do you need from me, your manager?

4. Reflect on any apprehension you have about being labeled a micromanager and consider if this fear has affected how you lead your team.

CHAPTER 3

Frustration #2—Delegation Disappointment: Why Aren't My Employees Doing What I Expect?

Managers know they must delegate, yet many fear letting go of the work. The fear leads to second-guessing and hesitation. And fear aside, most managers do not understand what it really takes to delegate, and to do it in a way that ensures high-quality work. Here is a conversation I had with a coaching client not long after I started my business.

Corina: Hi, how have things been going with your team since our last session?

Manager: Not bad, but I did run into

another frustrating situation. I delegated more tasks to my team like you suggested, but the results were disappointing. I even gave one employee a template to work from and he completely changed it, deleted critical sections, sent it back to me with the text in all different fonts. I could barely read it. It took me two hours to fix it. I feel like delegating takes longer. It's faster and easier to do it myself.

Corina: I understand your frustration. Did you give the employee any feedback on their work?

Manager: No, I didn't. That would have taken a while, to figure out how to have that conversation, so I just felt like it was easier to do it myself rather than dealing with the back-and-forth to get it right.

Corina: I appreciate your honesty. Delegation can be tricky, especially when quality and efficiency are at stake. First, I want to acknowledge your desire to maintain high standards. That's important. However, let's dive into what happened when you took the task back and completed it yourself. What message might your actions have sent to your employee?

Manager: I suppose it could have seemed like I didn't trust their abilities or that I didn't think they were capable of doing a good job.

Corina: Exactly. When we take tasks back

from our team members, especially after delegating them, it can inadvertently communicate a lack of trust or belief in their capabilities. This might lead to feelings of disengagement or demotivation for the employee. It's essential to find a balance between maintaining quality and fostering your team's growth.

Manager: But what if I delegate something important and it goes wrong? It could reflect badly on me.

Corina: I understand your concern. Let's consider a different perspective. Delegation is not just about getting tasks done; it's also about developing your team's skills and talents. Every member of your team has potential that can be unlocked through opportunities and challenges. While there's a risk that things might not go perfectly the first time, that's how growth happens. Remember, mistakes are part of the learning process.

Manager: That's true, but it can slow things down and be frustrating.

Corina: Yes, it can. Would you agree that doing something well often takes time?

Manager: Yes.

Corina: Successful delegation will require up-front effort. More than most managers realize. What if you start by clarifying expectations? Make sure the employee understands the task, its importance, and the desired outcome. Then, set clear parameters but also allow room for their creativity and problem-solving. When you delegated last time, did you take any of these steps?

Manager: No, not exactly. I gave the employee the data and the template and asked them to fill it in on the spreadsheet. It sounds like I left out a lot of details.

Corina: Most managers do unless they have developed a clear process for delegating every time. Did you conduct any check-ins where the employee could ask questions and you could provide an opportunity for guidance and feedback?

Manager: No. The employee returned the work to me, and I simply fixed it myself, so they probably think what they did was OK.

Corina: Exactly. Without feedback and direction, an employee has no idea that their work is not up to par. They think what they are doing is fine.

Manager: That makes sense. I guess I've been approaching delegation with the mindset that it's faster if I just do it myself rather than from the perspective that it's an opportunity to develop an employee.

Corina: I appreciate your honesty in sharing that. It's a common mindset problem managers must overcome. Remember, the goal isn't just to finish tasks but to build a capable and self-reliant team that can support you in achieving your broader goals.

Manager: You're right. I need to shift my perspective and give my team members more opportunities to shine.

Corina: I'm glad to hear that. As you continue to delegate, focus on the growth of your team members and the bigger picture. The idea is to start small and gradually increase the complexity of tasks you delegate.

WHAT IS THE REAL PROBLEM, AND WHY IS THIS FRUSTRATING?

The manager I coached in this scenario is experiencing what I call *delegation disappointment*. Delegation disappointment occurs when a manager delegates a task to an employee, walks away feeling good because they were able to get something off their plate, and then experiences crushing defeat when the work comes back to them incomplete or in poor quality.

There are many reasons managers experience this frustration. The primary reason for the disappointment and frustration is that the manager has an incomplete process for delegating. Much like the misunderstanding around micromanagement, most managers are not aware of how many steps are involved to delegate effectively to ensure they get the results they need beyond simply assigning a task to an employee. In this chapter, you will learn exactly what it takes to delegate work to an employee so they fully understand what is expected of them.

The second reason managers experience this frustration is because they thought they could "set it and forget it." Many managers are under the impression that delegating is simply assigning work to an employee and walking away. Managers must realize that, depending on the experience level of the employee and the complexity of the work, they will likely have to train, coach, and provide some level of support to the employee to help that employee build the competence they need to complete the work.

The third reason for delegation disappointment is that the manager *thinks* they are delegating, but their communication style is so passive it sounds more like a suggestion to an employee. On many occasions, a frustrated manager will look at me and say, "I *am* delegating! It's not working." When we take a closer look at how they are communicating, we realize they are making suggestions or recommendations but not *direct* requests. It sounds like this:

"You might want to . . ."
"It would be nice if you . . ."
"Maybe we should . . ."

Managers who do not fully own their leadership role or are uncomfortable with delegating tend to unknowingly soften their communication. The employee can hear this hesitation and is unlikely to follow through. Have you ever heard yourself delegating like this?

When managers make one or all of these delegation mistakes, they end up with employees on the team who are underutilized while the manager is still overworked. The *delegation disappointment* they feel leads them to believe that "it's faster and easier if I do it myself."

Delegating, when done right, is a force multiplier for a manager, their team, and the company. As the manager, you cannot focus on higher-level tasks if you are doing work your employees are being paid to do or if you are delegating but must jump in and fix the work. A manager who has not mastered delegating is ineffective, thereby limiting both their own career growth and the growth of their team. Team members cannot build competence if they are not given the opportunity to do the work or, when they do the work, their manager takes it back to fix it rather than give them the opportunity to learn from their mistakes. A company cannot grow when its managers become a bottleneck. And your employer is paying you to do your job, not the job of your employees. Remember, the only thing worse than not delegating effectively is not delegating *at all*. But that won't be an issue after you read this chapter.

SHIFT YOUR MINDSET AND LET GO OF THE WORK

The role of a manager is to facilitate the flow of work and to never become a bottleneck on the team. Nothing will slow down or impede that flow as quickly as a manager who won't let go of the work or who does not understand the full process of delegating. I understand why so many managers experience fear when it comes to letting go of the work. Managers don't want to look bad. They want to deliver work on time and of high quality. That fear that the work won't get done to the timeline and quality required. When it comes to delegating, we can get creative with the stories we tell ourselves about why we *shouldn't* let go of the work. There are telltale cues to help you assess and self-correct your management and communication style.

Here are my top three favorite lies we tell ourselves about why delegating won't work, and as a result, we restrict the flow of work on our teams:

1. "It's faster/easier if I do it myself."
2. "No one can do this work as well as I can."
3. "My employees are already so busy."

It *is* faster for you to do it, but only the first time. Then you are stuck doing work your employee could be doing and you begin to feel resentful that you are doing your employee's job. We might tell ourselves the story that no one can do this work as well as we can, but that is also not accurate. Our team members need the opportunity to build competence in their roles. And yes, your employees are busy, but why not ask them if they are able to take on more and prioritize the work with them?

Shift your mindset to get past the three "stories" we tell ourselves about why we can't delegate work to a team member. This will ensure you never become the bottleneck and employees won't become frustrated as they are underutilized.

Effective delegation requires two types of learning:

1. Shifting your mindset to create the habit of delegating. Doing everything yourself is your norm, and you've built the habit of fitting in every task in those "spare moments."
2. Learning the technical skills of delegating, such as how to communicate expectations effectively

and how to efficiently develop an employee to get the work done.

Just because you can do it yourself, doesn't mean you *should* do it yourself. You have an employee who is waiting to help you. They also want the opportunity to become competent in their job, but they can't do that if you won't delegate.

Shifting your mindset to realize that effective delegating is *up-front effort* for *long-term gain* is essential to mastering delegation. An employee will likely require development and resources to become competent in their role. This will take time, and it is worth it. It is not logical or feasible to keep taking back the work and fixing it or completing it yourself. So accepting the fact that there is a certain level of support required to ensure the work will be completed correctly will alleviate the disappointment and ensure you build a competent, high-performing team. If you have been telling yourself any of the stories I mentioned above, it is time to take a step back and reflect. Ask yourself, *What am I really afraid of?* Is it really about the fact that the work won't be completed the way you would do it, or is it that you like doing that work and feeling needed because only you can do it? Our internal motivations and need for recognition can fuel all sorts of fear about letting go of the work and letting someone else shine.

Once you have adjusted your mindset so you are ready to let go of the work, it is time to learn steps to delegate effectively and the tools and shortcuts that can make training employees easier so you can get your team where they need to be to complete the work effectively every time you delegate.

ASSIGN THE RIGHT TASK TO THE RIGHT EMPLOYEE

In my very first job out of university, my manager left for vacation, so our director asked me to write a proposal for a government grant to obtain funding, a task normally completed by my manager. I had never completed a task like this before. I had written plenty of papers for professors but never a proposal asking for something. I was too embarrassed to ask for help or admit that I didn't know how to complete the task. I was excited to have been assigned this level of responsibility. This is called *unconscious incompetence,* which is the point in a learning journey where you don't know what you don't know. If the proposal was ineffective, our department would have to cancel a project designed to support the career development of youth in the community. In other words, a high-risk task with big consequences for failure.

This task was a complete mismatch for the employee to whom it was assigned, and as you can guess, I failed miserably. I was too inexperienced and lacking in skill to complete this task. My inexperience also meant that I didn't know I could go back to my director and say, "This task is way over my head, and I need some help." My director set me, our department, and our stakeholders up for failure by not assessing whether the complexity and risk level of the task matched up with the skill and maturity level of the employee to whom she was assigning the work. Luckily, my manager came back from vacation, and we worked on the proposal together. She provided me with templates and examples and proofread everything before it was submitted.

There is nothing wrong with assigning a new task that an

employee doesn't know how to do yet. The key is to ensure the manager is there to provide the training, coaching, examples, and support the employee requires to complete the task.

I wish I could say that this situation I experienced at the beginning of my career was a one-off. But it happened in most of my jobs, and I frequently heard the same complaint from coworkers and, eventually, my clients. This approach is often justified with the common phrase "trial by fire" or the expression "Throw them in at the deep end (and they will learn how to swim)." But they might also drown.

There is a better way. Good managers strike a balance when assigning a task: allowing their teams to stretch their skills but preventing them from drowning or setting themselves on fire. You can do that by assessing the employee for their skill and maturity level and assessing how complex the task is with the level of risk associated if the employee fails.

If you are unsure about an employee's skill level or ability to handle a task or project, have a conversation with them. Once you have described the task or scope of work, have them rate their confidence about completing it on a scale from 1 to 10, with 10 being extremely confident and 1 being not at all confident. Ask, too, how they think they will approach the work. Their response will give you an idea of their skill level.

It can be challenging for an employee to admit they don't know how to do something they were hired to do. An employee's willingness to admit they don't know something often depends on the quality of the relationship they have with their manager. A good way to build this trust is to always admit when you don't know something or to share stories about some of the mistakes you've made in the past.

SETTING YOURSELF AND YOUR TEAM MEMBERS UP FOR SUCCESS

Most business and leadership influencers on the web focus solely on *what* a manager or business owner should delegate. The "$1,000 hour" activity, for instance, assigns a dollar value to tasks. The dollar value represents how much you could pay someone to do that task. The goal is that you do *only* the tasks that you consider to be of high value that *only* you can do. All the $10 and $100 tasks get delegated. This is a great exercise to help you understand what you can get off your plate. But it only helps you understand the *what* and not the *how*, a key source for delegation disappointment.

There are key steps you need to follow when delegating if you want to set yourself and your team members up for success. Most of those steps occur *before* you ever tell an employee what you would like them to do.

Before you ever delegate work to an employee, take a step back and consider four things:

1. **The skill level and maturity level of the employee.** Reflecting on the competence and experience level of the employee when delegating will help you approach delegating with realistic expectations. "Delegate it and forget it" rarely works in real life; most often, training and coaching is required to help an employee become competent at a particular task.
2. **The complexity of the task or work being assigned.** An employee can build confidence and

competence when they are assigned tasks that are incrementally challenging. An employee can feel defeated and inadequate if they are assigned work that is so far beyond their skill and experience, they don't even know where to begin.

3. **The risk associated with the work if the employee makes a mistake.** No one wants to make a costly mistake at work. I was assigned work several times throughout my career I was not ready for, and the consequences of not completing the work correctly could have been dire had my manager not stepped in to provide support. A modern manager considers the level of risk associated with the work if the employee makes a mistake. This is not permission to "take back the work and do it yourself." It is an opportunity to evaluate the consequences and reflect on whether the employee responsible for the work is supported.

4. **The employee's readiness to take ownership of a task.** If you truly want to keep work off your plate, you will have to also delegate ownership of the work to the employee. If an employee is doing their work but not taking initiative beyond what is asked of them, it could be a sign that they do not feel a sense of ownership over their role. Assigning work to an employee is not enough to encourage ownership. You also must delegate authority an employee will require to make the work their own.

This can be accomplished in several ways. You can communicate to an employee that you expect them to take the initiative to improve their work. Provide details about the level of responsibility they have to make decisions about their work. For example, a customer service manager client was overwhelmed with the amount of texts and calls she was getting from customer service agents on the evening shift. The agents were asking her how to deal with upset customers and seeking permission to provide a complimentary service to appease unhappy customers.

I suggested that the manager allow her agents to use their discretion and offer a free service up to a certain amount without checking in with her. The manager implemented this process for a trial period, and it was effective in providing more autonomy to the employees and reduced demands on her time.

Work will likely end up back on your plate when you don't factor in these considerations. We are all busy, and it can seem unrealistic to take this time for a more mindful approach to delegating. When you consider how much of your time is taken up with fixing work or doing your employee's job, the return on that time becomes evident.

MAKE THE IMPLICIT EXPLICIT

A key, often overlooked, strategy that must be included when you delegate is expectation setting. If you want to create a work environment where employees can perform at their best, don't make employees guess what is expected of them. Be the kind of manager that frees up the headspace of your employees by always keeping them informed and letting them know what the priorities are. Setting clear expectations about the work will improve employee performance and productivity by reducing the confusion and time spent by employees trying to figure out what their manager wants from them.

Some conscientious employees can spend a lot of time and concern worrying or wondering what their manager is thinking. Make the implicit explicit. Do not assume your team members are always aware of an expectation that you have not communicated or that they know every aspect of their job for which they have not been thoroughly trained.

An example of effective expectation setting is telling your team member how you expect them to deal with challenges they encounter in their work and where you want them to go for help. Setting deadlines is another example of expectation setting, as is discussing how often you and a team member will meet for updates on their work.

When a manager is skilled and knowledgeable on a task and the work comes easily to them, it is simple to think that it will also be easy for the employee. This assumption can cause more frustration for both the employee and the manager. The employee can feel like they have not been properly trained or expectations are not clear. The manager may be left scratching their head, wondering why the employee wasn't able to complete an apparently easy task. A technique you can use to support an employee and evaluate if they are on the right track with their assigned work is called a *milestone check-in*. This technique is helpful when an employee has less experience with the work or if there is a level of uncertainty or complexity. When you assign a task, you tell the employee you would like to have a check-in with them when they have completed 25 percent of the work, 50 percent of the work, and then when the work is completed. This can sound like a lot of oversight, but you won't have to ask an employee to check in with you this frequently once they are fully competent and confident in their role. You can continue with milestone check-ins in at 25 percent, 50 percent, and 100 percent completion until an employee is consistently producing high-quality work.

Many employees prefer to present completed work because they don't want their manager to see their "sloppy first draft." If an employee resists regular check-ins, remind them that it's better to check in and ensure things are on the right track than to wait until they think they are finished and the final product is not what is required. Milestone check-ins also help a manager and an employee learn how to communicate with each other. This approach of *up-front effort for long-term gain* is worth it because you will build competence in your team members and you can trust that the work will get done.

Another technique that accompanies milestone check-ins is a two-part process called *gradual increase in responsibility* and *gradual release of responsibility*. Successfully developing an employee typically means a manager will provide more training, coaching, and guidance when a task is first assigned or when an employee initially joins a team, and gradually they will reduce that support when the employee is competent and confident in their abilities. The employee will experience a gradual increase in responsibility as they are ready, and the manager will experience a gradual decrease in responsibility as the employee builds competence in their role. When an employee is consistently completing or producing high-quality work, a manager can finally delegate and walk away.

All Managers Are CROs

Does it ever feel like no matter how many employees you hire, you still end up with more work than you can handle? If so, step back and look at your own communication skills, and ask yourself, in particular: *Am I underestimating how often I will have to repeat myself?*

Organizational health and leadership expert Patrick Lencioni coined the CRO title to remind managers that there is no such thing as "too much communication." CRO stands for "chief reminding officer," and according to Lencioni, all managers are CROs. Though we don't want to appear as micromanagers, most employees need to hear key messages several times before they sink in. Effective CROs remind their teams about the following:

- the purpose of their work;
- your expectations for how they will perform;
- the company's expectations for everyone;
- priorities for the day, week, and month; and
- your boundaries. Yes, managers can have boundaries.

"I am tired of repeating myself," many managers exclaim. But the sooner they embrace their chief reminding officer title, the sooner they begin to ensure work flows through them, instead of stopping with them, and the sooner they step into their leadership role with more patience and empathy.

Recognizing what your employees are going through is an antidote to delegation disappointment. Put yourself in your employees' shoes: they are juggling multiple priorities, multiple communication channels, and requests from you, their team, their colleagues, and maybe even customers. Plus, they have their own personal issues, concerns, and plans.

They are going to forget things sometimes. In a world of constant interruption, it takes world-class organizational skills to stay on top of things. It is safe to say that we could all be more organized and track information more effectively.

SUPPORT YOUR DELEGATION EFFORTS WITH SYSTEMS AND PROCESSES

All managers will have to repeat key expectations to team members, and there are things you can do that will set yourself and your team up for success:

1. Create written processes for *every* task that gets repeated more than twice.

Reduce occurrences of mundane tasks being forgotten and the need to repeat yourself by documenting the step-by-step process for completing the task. Ask an employee to document their steps when completing repeatable tasks and provide autonomy to create their own set of processes for their role. Checklists are a good example of a documented process. When you use a public washroom in a gas station, you might notice the checklist on the wall outlining the checkpoints for cleaning the washroom. Human error can be minimized significantly with such a simple tool. My client Marieke Gow, who owns the Artisan Inn and Twine Loft in picturesque Trinity, Newfoundland and Labrador, devised a checklist for the employees who clean the rooms at the inn after a situation where a bathroom didn't get cleaned well. This simple tool improved teamwork and increased accountability. Employees were happier because they had clarity over their roles and what was expected of them. The transparency created from having a checklist with clearly assigned roles and tasks also cut out any option to pass blame if a task was missed.

2. Record training sessions, and create a resource library.

Training an employee is necessary but can also be time-consuming. A quick tip to cut training time is to ensure you record every training session you have with an employee. You can create an evergreen training system by using tools like Loom and a voice-to-text app on your phone or your computer. These are two of the best tools for creating training sessions for employees. If you know you will need to train an employee in the task you are doing, open Loom and do a desktop recording as you work. Talk out loud and record exactly how you are doing each step. Open a Word doc or an email. Turn on Dictate or the little microphone on your keyboard and record step-by-step instructions for an employee on how to complete a task. Ask the employee you are training to write up the instructions as a standard operating procedure (SOP).

I have encountered many businesses that do not have documented systems and processes and have no idea where to start in creating them. A lack of written processes or SOPs means managers do not have a system in place for quickly training an employee on a task and turning that training session into an evergreen training system for future employees.

3. Create a visual tracking system.

All managers must understand workflow, systems, and productivity to get the most out of their team and their time. Once you have a team to lead, you no longer need to know how to do all the work—you need to understand how to create an efficient workflow and systems to support your team members to do their work. As a business owner, I have always found that a visual tool or representation of workflow is essential to ensuring everyone stays on top of their workload. A visual tool always cuts down on the need to ask for updates because team members post their updates directly in the tool.

There are many online tools that can be used to create a visual dashboard to keep tabs on work that has yet to be assigned, is in progress, on pause, or completed. Project management tools like Asana and Trello are helpful.

Depending on the type of work you do, the volume of work, and the size of your team, you may be able to use something simple such as an Excel spreadsheet to track projects, assignments, updates, and deadlines.

A delegation dashboard is a tool I advise my clients to create to keep track of the work they have yet to assign; work they have already assigned, along with its stage of completion; work that is on pause and why it's paused; and completed work.

A visual delegation dashboard has many benefits. Aside from helping employees keep track of the work they have been assigned, it also creates a culture of accountability on the team. The visual dashboard makes it clear who is responsible for what, when the work is due, and the rate of progress being made. Each employee will also know who to go to if they have questions about a particular project or task without having to check in with their manager.

A visual dashboard or document that clearly states all the tasks each employee on your team is responsible for is a useful way to help team members keep track of roles and progress. It also fosters peer accountability. A RACI chart is a responsibility assignment matrix frequently used in project management.[9] RACI stands for responsible, accountable, consulted, and informed. Team members will understand who needs to work together to get something done once the RACI chart is completed. You can create your own version of a responsibility assignment matrix with your team if RACI is not a fit for the work you are doing. There are a number of free RACI matrix templates available online.

The workloads of managers and employees are heavier than ever, and it can be a challenge to remember every little thing that must get done in a day. The more tasks and procedures an employee is expected to remember each day, the more important it is to have some version of a delegation dashboard.

DON'T BENCH YOUR PLAYERS

In the ninth grade, I joined my high school basketball team. I was hardly on my way to playing professionally, but what I lacked in natural talent, I made up for in passion and energy. It was our only tournament for the year, and I couldn't wait to play against another team.

My excitement quickly turned to disappointment when my coach *benched* me the entire tournament. I distinctly remember her words as she looked at me sitting on the bench: "I must go with my more experienced players."

It was high school basketball. The goal should have been to give the rookies some much-needed experience on the court and give everyone the opportunity to practice working as a team. But she just wanted to win. We didn't win. It wasn't even a close game.

Our coach was leading with fear. As a result, we all lost. I see a similar dynamic play out in workplaces every day.

Not giving your employees a chance to develop and grow is a morale killer.

Busy, overworked managers want to delegate work to team members. Maybe they have delegated in the past, but the work came back to them incomplete, late, or of lower quality. Or maybe they perceive that the stakes are too high, so they tell themselves stories like *It's just faster and easier if I do it myself.*

The solution is for managers to learn *all the steps* that go into getting the performance they need from their team, and delegating is only one part of that "performance puzzle." Knowing how to delegate and set expectations effectively is a key piece of that puzzle.

Don't bench your employees—give them a chance to develop into the star players you know they can be by learning the skills you need to bring out the best in them! With clear communication, clarity of role, and an evergreen training system, managers can expect good results when they delegate. If you have done everything possible on your end to communicate effectively and set an employee up for success and you do not see an improvement, then it might be time for a conversation with the employee about whether their job is a good fit for them. I will cover that process in the next two chapters. If an employee doesn't seem to care about their work or doing it well, then you might be dealing with an attitude problem.

END-OF-CHAPTER REFLECTION, EXERCISES, AND TOOLS:

1. For the next week, write down each task you complete on a Post-it note or in a notebook. At the end of the week, evaluate each task as to whether it is in your job description and scope or that of one of your team members. This activity will help you assess whether you are doing your own job or your employee's job.
2. Design a delegation dashboard the next two times you delegate a task to an employee. Reflect on whether you have delegated and communicated this level of detail and clarity in the past. If the

answer is no, reflect on whether some of the disappointment you have experienced when you delegated a task to an employee is because of the way you communicated the directive.
3. In your next 1:1 with each team member who reports to you, ask them if you have been providing enough information when you delegate.

CHAPTER 4

Frustration #3— Feedback Fiasco: How to Prevent Feedback Conversations from Going Sideways

No one can improve their performance without quality feedback, yet many managers avoid conversations where they must inform an employee that their performance is not up to par, their behavior or attitude needs adjustment, or they made a mistake. These conversations can be difficult, but Adam Grant, best-selling author and organizational psychologist at Wharton, captured the real consequence of avoidance in a LinkedIn post: "Withholding feedback is choosing comfort over growth. Staying silent deprives people of the opportunity to learn. If you're worried about hurting their feelings, it's a sign you haven't earned their trust. In healthy relationships, honesty is an expression of care."

I have trained and coached many managers on how to give effective constructive and positive feedback, and the following conversation stands out in my mind most often when I helped a frustrated manager see the real value of delivering constructive feedback to an employee.

> **Corina:** So, tell me about your team. How many team members do you have, and how are they performing?
>
> **Manager:** I have three team members. Two are amazing and what I consider high performers. And I have one team member whom I always need to stay on top of to get anything from him.
>
> **Corina:** Interesting. Have you given the team member who you need to stay on top of any feedback, or have you had a conversation to find out what is going on?
>
> **Manager:** I have had some conversations with him, and I asked him some questions to find out more about him and how he is motivated. I am not sure he actually wants this role, and I got the impression he might be looking for a different job.
>
> **Corina:** That's also interesting. What approach do you think you should take with him?

Manager: I am not sure. I know that if I keep giving more work to the high performers, they might leave. They see he is not pulling his weight. But if he is leaving, what is the point in starting a conversation about his performance?

Corina: You are right. High performers won't tolerate underperformance going unchecked. No one wants to have to pull the weight of someone else. But he hasn't put in his notice yet, so he could still be with you for a while—correct?

Manager: Yes.

Corina: What is the impact of his performance on you?

Manager: I am resentful that I must check in with him so often, and I have stopped delegating because I don't have faith that the work will get done. The work is piling up for me, and I am feeling stressed.

Corina: I bet. This team member's performance is affecting you and your team. Even if he moves on, wouldn't it be better to help him become aware that he can't just check out while he is here?

Manager: Yes. The longer this goes on, the greater the risk I could lose one of my other team members.

Corina: I agree. Let's work through where

you can start with a feedback conversation with this team member.

Manager: I was thinking about getting curious and asking him how he thinks he is doing. Perhaps I should also evaluate how I have been communicating and delegating as well. Maybe I am not clearly communicating deadlines and expectations.

Corina: I think that is a good place to start. We never want to begin these conversations with blame. Curiosity is key. What will you do if he thinks he is doing well and is not aware of his own performance?

Manager: I will tell him that I must check in with him frequently to remind him about the work I have asked him to do. I will ask him if I am not communicating deadlines clearly enough and set an expectation that I would like him to check in with me if he is running into issues.

Corina: I think that's good. It's a good idea to reflect on our communication style and ask what we could be doing better. Remember, leadership is not just about giving feedback; it's also about guiding and supporting your team members on their journey to improvement. Keep working with this team member, and over time you'll likely see the positive changes you're looking for.

WHAT IS THE REAL PROBLEM, AND WHY IS THIS FRUSTRATING?

Sixty-five percent of employees want more feedback, and companies that implement consistent feedback conversations with employees experience 14.9 percent lower turnover rates.[10] Eighty percent of employees who say they have received meaningful feedback in the past week are fully engaged.[11] Feedback conversations are a powerful tool in any manager's toolbox for inspiring the best possible performance from an employee or colleague. Yet many managers are not using this tool to build stronger teams and achieve greater outcomes. Or when they attempt to give feedback, the conversation turns into what I call a *feedback fiasco*. Before I define a feedback fiasco and explain why it occurs, it is helpful to explain the two different types of feedback known as *constructive* and *positive feedback*.

1. *Constructive feedback* is a specific comment based on observations by the manager regarding behavior or technical performance that can be improved. The manager will also provide insight or support to the employee to improve performance.
2. *Positive feedback* is a comment that affirms or recognizes past behavior or performance. It focuses on behavior and actions that were successful and should be continued.

Some workplaces and managers still refer to constructive feedback as "critical feedback" or "negative feedback." The words we use matter, and referring to feedback as critical or negative will change the perceived value of the feedback and possibly put someone on edge before they even hear the feedback. I recommend only using the word *constructive* to describe feedback on a mistake or required improvement.

A feedback fiasco is when a manager does any of the following:

- avoids giving feedback of any kind, constructive or positive, to a team member, thereby stalling the growth of the employee and the team;
- abdicates responsibility for giving feedback by asking someone else to give the team member constructive feedback, such as Human Resources or another team member;
- delivers constructive feedback to an employee and receives a negative reaction from the employee;
- delivers constructive feedback and the employee appears to accept the feedback but does not change their behavior or performance; and/or
- delivers feedback in a way that is vague and not actionable, resulting in no change in performance.

The goal of effective constructive feedback is to *inspire* a change of some kind such as a higher level of performance from the person receiving the feedback. The goal of effective positive feedback is to *inspire* continued good performance and offer recognition. If any of the above scenarios occur, it means the manager has the impression that feedback conversations are not worth it, are difficult, and should be avoided, or has not received training on how to communicate high-quality feedback. Poorly constructed or delivered feedback or no feedback at all will leave an employee feeling confused about their performance and disengaged in their role.

THE ORIGIN OF THE FEEDBACK FIASCO

There are many reasons for feedback fiascos. Many managers struggle with feedback conversations because they don't understand the point of feedback, they are worried about the reaction of the employee, or they are more worried about being liked than being effective as a manager.

Missing the Point of Feedback

I was coaching an experienced manager who had developed a habit of coming up with work-arounds to deal with the underperformance of a particular team member. When I asked him why he spent so much time figuring out how to compensate for his team member's mistakes, he responded, "Who am I to tell someone they are doing something wrong?" I get that we are all human and we all make mistakes, even managers. When a team member isn't performing or makes a mistake, it can feel hard to point out their mistakes when you've probably made a few of your own. This manager is experiencing a feedback fiasco because he doesn't see the value or understand the point of constructive feedback. It's not about pointing out someone's mistakes. It's about giving the employees the information they need to perform at their best. And the longer a manager waits to do that, the worse the employee will feel about the mistake they've been making.

I explained to my client that by *not* giving this employee the constructive feedback they clearly needed, the manager was hurting the employee's career. The employee would likely never get the opportunity to take on more responsibility in their current role since they were not performing effectively with their current tasks. And if they did move on to another role or company, they would take these bad habits and underperformance with them, which would reflect on the leadership of their previous manager and employer. As you can see, there is a negative ripple effect on the employee and their manager when constructive feedback is withheld. When an employee doesn't receive feedback of any type, constructive or positive, they assume what they are doing is working.

Avoidance and Abdication

Asking someone else to deliver constructive feedback to an employee when that employee reports directly to you is also not acceptable. I have observed managers abdicate responsibility in this area, and it demonstrates a lack of leadership and care for their team. I understand that constructive-feedback conversations can be challenging. Focusing on the possibility of improving performance for both the employee and the team and improving the relationship can help a manager get past feelings of fear and discomfort.

Managers may also avoid constructive-feedback conversations because they are worried about the reaction of the employee. Perhaps the employee has reacted negatively in the past to constructive feedback or the manager had a bad experience in the past with a feedback conversation. I will explain how to deliver constructive feedback in a way that is less likely to ignite a negative reaction in the next section. What managers must remember, however, is that they are not responsible for the reaction of their team members. We are all adults, and therefore responsible for how we show up for work each day and how we respond to information whether we asked for that information or not. If an employee consistently reacts in a negative way to constructive feedback, then it is time to have a conversation just on that topic and set the expectation that feedback is essential to effective performance. I will provide an example of how to address a negative reaction to constructive feedback in the next section.

Wanting to Be Liked

Sometimes, when a manager is worried about the reaction to constructive feedback, it is not because they think the employee will become defensive or aggressive. They are worried their team members will no longer like them. These are the concerns of a *nice* manager who strives to make everyone on the team happy and therefore exhibits people-pleasing behavior. Remember, it is not a manager's job to make everyone "happy." You are not ice cream. In my experience, people-pleasing often leads to avoidance of difficult conversations and not giving constructive feedback when needed out of fear the employee will become upset or not like you. In this situation, it is helpful to understand the difference between being the *nice* manager and the *kind* manager.

Kindness is doing something that is helpful to others. Kind managers give constructive feedback and have tough conversations because they know the damage it can do to an employee's career (and the progress of the team) if they allow poor performance to persist. After all, we can't improve or fix something we are not aware of. Recognizing that withholding constructive feedback can often cause more damage to an employee's career is often the biggest mindset shift required to help someone fully step into their role as a manager. When a kind manager is delivering constructive feedback or having a difficult conversation, their intentions are always about making things better for the employee and team. They don't blame or shame the employee. And they frame the feedback in a way that makes it useful for the employee. The *nice* manager is more concerned with being liked, being friends with them, and making everyone on the team happy. You can't *lead* and people please at the same time. Leaders make decisions based on what is needed, not what everyone wants. A nice manager can also be motivated by wanting to jump in and save their employees to be viewed as a hero for their team. Be a leader who develops others, not the manager who jumps in to save them.

The Feedback Is Subjective and Not Actionable

Useful, constructive feedback tells the employee exactly what they need to improve upon in a way that is objective, concrete, and actionable. If you have delivered constructive feedback and the employee seems to accept the feedback but does not change their behavior or performance, this is a sign that the feedback may not have been as actionable and specific as you think it was.

Women often receive a particularly useless piece of feedback: "You need to be more confident." A manager typically provides this feedback if the team member is not speaking up and sharing their ideas in meetings. It's easy to fall into the trap of simply telling an employee to "be" someone or something else. On the surface, this type of feedback appears useful, but it can be discouraging for the employee. People cannot just decide to "be" something or someone else.

You may have an employee whom you know is intelligent and who has a lot of ideas to contribute but doesn't speak up in meetings. It would be easy to assume this employee is lacking in confidence, prompting their manager to give them feedback that they "need to be more confident and speak up more often in meetings." A good manager would strive to understand why an employee is behaving in a specific way. They would ask the employee a question, such as "You have shared some great ideas with me in our one-on-ones. I am curious why you don't speak up more in meetings and share your thoughts." Perhaps the meetings are so chaotic the employee is struggling to get a word in. The employee may be unsure of their ideas, but simply telling them to be more confident will not help.

A more effective way of delivering this feedback sounds like this, "I have noticed that you are hesitating to speak up in meetings and share your ideas. Your ideas are good, and we hired you to help us turn this project around. How can I support you in meetings so you feel more comfortable speaking up?"

Next, a good manager would proceed to coach the employee if the employee is open to being coached, because coaching is the most effective way to unlock new behaviors and help someone reach their potential. You can read about simple coaching techniques in the next chapter.

If constructive feedback is vague or not actionable, the employee likely won't see the value in changing and they may not understand the impact of their behavior. Some employees will improve their behavior as soon as their manager suggests a change, but most will need a reason to change. Connecting the feedback and the desired change in behavior to something that is important to the employee, such as career growth, will ignite the intrinsic motivation the employee will need to put in the effort to change. Second, letting an employee know why you are giving them feedback also lets the employee know that you are not simply picking on them or being the overbearing manager. The "why" must be related to something that is important to the employee.

Focusing on Personality

We can ask someone to change their attitude, behavior, or actions, but we cannot ask someone to change their personality. A common situation I have been asked to help clients with is the clash of personalities between two team members. Typically, one team member is quiet, introverted, or values politeness. The other employee might be extroverted, forceful in their communication, or value directness. These two types of employees always seem to struggle to get along.

While it might be a personality clash causing the conflict, it would be unfair to ask either employee to change who they are. A manager can't ask an employee to be less extroverted or less introverted. This is not something a person can change. You will paint yourself into a corner by focusing on the personality of an employee or coworker. A manager can focus on communication style or behavior such as "being disruptive." A manager could ask an employee to be more considerate of the needs of others in the office. A manager could also use the opportunity to help each employee recognize that diversity of personalities and communication styles is a good thing, and team members can complement each other in work style and skill set. For feedback to be effective, it must focus on skills or behaviors that an employee can change, such as communication style.

I have heard "It's just who they are" as an excuse for the behavior and performance of many employees and managers. Typically, this justification is used on someone who is strong in technical performance but lacking in people skills and is offending coworkers while alienating themselves. Assess the issue from the perspective of what skills or behaviors must improve to become a well-rounded employee who is effective in their role and with their coworkers. In some instances, a performance problem masking as a personality issue occurs with an employee who is a positive, happy person, but they do not produce high-quality work. I was delivering a talk on accountability to a roomful of executives when one of them asked me how to deal with an employee who was, in his words, a ray of sunshine but missing some key skills required for their role. The executive assumed giving this employee constructive feedback meant he would sound like he was disparaging her bright personality, which he considered an asset to the culture. I advised him to provide recognition for her positive attitude as well as feedback on the areas needing improvement. Personality did not even need to be mentioned. In this scenario, his dialogue might start like this:

Manager: "Your positive attitude is an asset to the organization. I have received messages from clients about how great it is to work with you. There are several technical areas in your skill set that, if improved, would make you unstoppable in your career. I would be happy to support you in gaining those skills if you are open-minded to the idea of training."

Effective feedback comes with suggestions for improvement and the offer of support. It is also important to remember how adults learn when initiating feedback conversations. Adults learn and develop best when their manager recognizes the knowledge and skills the employee is bringing to the table and can connect new behavior and expectations to that existing expertise.

GETTING PAST THE FEAR OF FEEDBACK CONVERSATIONS

Initiating a constructive-feedback conversation can bring up many emotions, especially fear. It is natural to fear the unknown. You don't know how the employee will react or what the impact will be on the relationship once you have the conversation.

A former coaching client whom I will call Tom reached out to me for help because employee morale was low in his department. The company had gone through changes and growth, resulting in external hiring and several internal promotions. One employee on his team applied for several internal promotions but was unsuccessful, and Tom could see the impact not moving ahead in their role was having on their attitude and level of engagement.

I asked Tom if anyone provided feedback to the unsuccessful applicant as to why they were not receiving a new role. Tom replied that the company typically did not provide feedback to internal applicants, and this situation was even more complicated because, according to Tom's assessment, this employee would never be suitable for a management role. I suggested that the right thing to do would be to have a meeting with the employee and help them understand why they were not suitable for the role so they could work on the areas where they needed to improve. Tom protested and assumed no good could come from that conversation. He said he'd attempted to give the employee feedback once before and it ended with the employee getting defensive, which is one of the reasons he was not considered for a promotion in the first place.

I empathized with Tom. It is not easy to explain to someone why they are not the right person for a role, but I asked him to consider the alternative. The morale and engagement of this employee had already decreased. If no one invested any time or belief in this employee by providing constructive feedback, the employee would likely move on and take a bad impression of the organization with him. Even worse, he might stay and influence others with this low morale.

I asked Tom to prepare some thoughts and feedback he could provide to this employee. It took Tom a few days to reflect on feedback that would be useful to this employee and to get past his discomfort. With some guidance from me, Tom invited the employee to a conversation.

"I realize you applied for several internal positions and were unsuccessful in your attempts to move ahead in your career," he said to the employee. "I realize that must have been disappointing. I would be happy to sit down with you and provide some insight as to why you were not chosen for those roles, brainstorm options for your career here, and create a development plan that could help you prepare for future opportunities."

The employee agreed to the conversation, and while there was some defensiveness in his tone, he did see the conversation as an investment in his future. Tom had been concerned about dealing with the defensiveness, and I informed him that it is not his responsibility to manage the employee's emotions. It is, however, an opportunity to discuss the employee's behavior and how it affected his opportunities to move ahead.

Tom and I reflected on how he felt during the conversation with the employee. He recognized that avoiding constructive-feedback conversations typically makes a situation worse. He also realized that feeling uncomfortable during a difficult constructive-feedback conversation doesn't mean the conversation should not be occurring. Those emotions mean that there is something important at stake, the relationship and the employee's future, and care must be taken to plan the conversation.

Modern managers manage their emotions when faced

with challenging conversations. You can acknowledge how you feel and accept that some conversations will be more difficult than others. The benefits of initiating these important conversations, however, outweigh the discomfort and uncertainty.

Can't I Just Use AI?

When I hear that managers are turning to AI to write their performance reviews, I get chills (not the good kind!). New technology has always held so much potential to transform how we work. But using AI to support key people functions of management can be problematic.

Only people can engage people. If you want to use ChatGPT to revise a written performance review to help you organize your thoughts, fine. I, however, am trying to get companies to move away from formal yearly reviews and encourage managers to have real conversations with their team members. This is especially important when an employee's performance is not up to par.

I have received many calls from frantic employees who were blindsided by their performance review. Rather than have ongoing, face-to-face conversations with them, their manager decided to save up all the constructive feedback and put it in writing to deliver it right before their yearly performance review. I can see why any worker would be devastated to receive

> feedback in that way. With the increasing uses of technology in our workplaces, we must hold on to our humanity wherever possible. World crisis after world crisis is telling us that we do not need more technology when engaging with each other; we need to hold on to our humanity, especially when we communicate with one another. Also, when we don't use our skills, we lose our skills. Relying on ChatGPT or other AI tools makes our own communication skills dull and blunt.

HOW TO DELIVER EFFECTIVE, ACTIONABLE FEEDBACK

I received a distraught call from someone seeking my help as a leadership coach early one morning. When the vibes are as fevered as this, I know that something has happened at work and I'm being sought after for remedial and reactive, not proactive, guidance.

I asked him why he reached out. "My board members are unhappy with my communication style," he told me. "They said my style comes across as if I am not taking my job seriously. They told me I need to change . . . or else!" In other words, he would be fired if he didn't quickly change his style.

I asked him how long his board members had felt this way and he said at least *a year*. I felt for the guy. No one should be blindsided with the "change or else" ultimatum. Unfortunately, many managers and business owners withhold constructive feedback for a long time. Sometimes even saving it up for that one-year performance review.

I understand how difficult it can be to tell someone they are doing something wrong or could be doing better. What is important to remember is that no one can improve their performance without feedback. Shifting your mindset from seeing constructive feedback as a negative situation to seeing it as an opportunity for growth can provide relief from the discomfort of constructive-feedback conversations.

The intention and spirit of feedback should always be about helping someone improve to grow themselves and their career. If someone approached me and said, "I have some negative feedback for you about your last presentation," I am not sure I would be thrilled to hear it. If, however, someone said, "I have some thoughts on how you could improve your next presentation that might get you more sales," I would be all ears. The purpose and value of the feedback for me is clear, and I would want to hear what the person had to say.

The following framework will help any manager organize their thoughts before starting a feedback conversation to deliver the feedback in a way that will encourage the employee to accept and use the feedback:

- *Circumstances*
- *Performance*
- *Impact*
- *Why*

You outline the *circumstances* as you observed them

without blame. Then, state the behavior or action (*performance*) that might be causing the problem. Next, let the person know the *impact* you are concerned about. Lastly, explain *why* you are giving them feedback in a way that lets them know you care about their career and progress.

Here are some examples of C.P.I.—*Why* in action.

Let's say a manager of a sales team tagged along in a meeting with a sales rep. During the meeting the sales rep talked over the potential client and didn't answer the prospect's questions. When the meeting ended and they were returning to the office, the conversation might go like this:

> **Manager:** So, how do you think that went?
>
> **Sales rep:** Good, I think I got the key points across.
>
> **Manager:** Yes, you did. Are you open to some feedback on how that meeting could have gone even better?
>
> **Sales rep:** Sure.
>
> **Manager:** The prospect didn't give us a final answer, so it will likely take another meeting to close the deal (*circumstances*). I noticed you interrupted the prospect once when they were trying to ask a question. And I am not sure you fully addressed her last concern about ROI (*performance*). I am concerned the prospect might not feel heard and valued (*impact*).
>
> **Sales rep:** I didn't see it that way at all, but I guess I could slow down in these meetings.

I have been told in the past that I interrupt people, so maybe I need to pay more attention to the other person. I sort of see these meetings as more of a sales presentation than a conversation.

Manager: That's a great insight. Do you think these types of meetings would go better if you viewed them as a conversation rather than a presentation?

Sales rep: Well, there is only one way to find out. I can give it a try and see if my close rates improve.

Manager: That sounds like a great plan. I am giving you this feedback because I see how passionate you are about your role, and I know with a few tweaks you could see an exponential improvement in your results, which can only benefit your career (*why*).

Sales rep: Thank you. I'm glad you see how passionate I am about getting our clients the products they need to grow their business.

This example is a best-case scenario, meaning the employee didn't get defensive and came to their own conclusion about their performance. Your conversations might not go quite so straightforward. However, if you stick to the same structure for feedback conversations, eventually your team members will know what to expect from these types of conversations. Explaining the impact an employee's actions are having on themselves or the team *and* telling the employee *why* you are giving them feedback are two key ingredients for effective feedback that get missed by most managers.

Feedback is subjective. When I share these examples in my keynote talks and trainings, I have had audience members remark that the structure sounds like sugarcoating or that I am dancing around the issue. Other times, I have had attendees remark that these examples are too harsh, and they would cry if someone gave them this feedback. If your company and its managers have a communication style that is aggressive, yes, I can see why anything less than aggressive would look like sugarcoating. The approach I train and coach on for delivering feedback isn't sugarcoating—it's a diplomatic and respectful communication style. It's a process and style that encourages accountability while placing a priority on maintaining the relationship. Aggressive communication is the easy way. Anyone can do it. It requires no self-control.

The point here is that every employee and colleague you work with will have different thresholds for the level of constructive feedback they can handle. This doesn't mean managers should shy away from giving employees constructive feedback. It means you will have to pay attention to how each employee responds during these conversations and adjust your communication style for each employee.

For instance, in my previous example, a manager was giving feedback to a sales rep. People working in sales typically receive a lot of feedback on their performance in the form of conversations but also by having their metrics posted alongside their team members'. In this situation, a manager may be able to deliver constructive feedback in a more direct way. Another employee may not be accustomed to receiving constructive feedback, so the manager will have to consider the best way to deliver direct feedback to someone who may not respond well.

Managers should also create a habit of catching employees doing something right. The behavior that gets recognized gets repeated. Consider the "class clown" in high school. We all know the student who acted up because they wanted attention from the teacher, and they got it. So recognize the type of performance you want to see more of. In the scenario with the sales rep, if I were this person's manager, I would tag along again in a few months, and if I noticed that the sales rep had changed their behavior for the better, I would be sure to provide positive feedback. It might sound like this:

> I noticed you have really changed your approach to conducting these sales calls. You are much more conversational and are listening to the prospect. The prospect clearly responded well because you closed the sale in just one meeting. The fact that you were willing to accept feedback and use it to improve your work tells me you are a team player, and you have a willingness to improve. I would recommend you to my manager for taking on higher-profile clients if that is what you want.

It is just as important to be specific when delivering positive feedback and explain the *why* of the feedback to the employee to make the feedback meaningful and useful. In this situation, the manager is asking the employee if it is valuable to them if they recommend the employee take on higher-profile clients. It's nice to receive a "good job" from our manager or a colleague, but to hear the impact we are having is more meaningful and more likely to increase morale and engagement.

Effective feedback conversations are an essential tool for helping everyone in a company improve performance and develop into the best version of themselves. Remember the HR manager I mentioned in chapter 2, Michelle? While Michelle has two high performers and one good-and-improving performer on her team, she has one other HR assistant who has been struggling in their role, whom we will call Robert. This HR assistant has a formal education in human resources but came from a role in the not-for-profit sector, where he was working directly with a vulnerable population. It didn't take long for Michelle to see that Robert was not connected to his role. She would assign work to him, and it would not get done. Michelle would constantly have to ask for updates.

Before having a conversation with Robert about his performance, Michelle reflected on everything she learned about management styles, delegating, and assessing performance from my program. Thinking about the Manager's Scale, she wondered if she was providing enough oversight and support to Robert. After all, even though Robert is formally educated in human resources, he has never actually worked in a HR role. After thoroughly assessing how her communication and management style might be affecting Robert's performance, she decided to initiate a feedback conversation with him.

Michelle approached the conversation from a place of curiosity and gave Robert plenty of time to tell his story. She reminded him that he was not completing his work as required and asked him what was going on. Michelle's initial suspicions were correct: Robert needed more direction. This was his first human resource role, after all. He was unsure about many of the tasks, was not feeling confident yet. Michelle immediately began communicating with specificity each time she delegated a task to Robert. She became concrete with her instruction and expectations until Robert was feeling more confident in his role.

Figuring out why an employee's performance is not up to par can take time, and it can require conversations that might feel awkward. But the outcome can be worth the temporary discomfort. Many managers who come through my programs are terrified of giving constructive feedback to an employee because they are focused on the part where they must tell someone they did something wrong or are not doing something they should be doing. Moving past this discomfort requires a mindset shift to see feedback conversations as an opportunity to remove performance roadblocks and gain a better understanding of how an employee needs to be supported by you, their manager.

Knowing how to give effective, useful feedback to your team members is a game changer. It is also my experience that most managers believe they are providing useful, effective feedback to their employees but are missing the boat on the specificity and intention of the feedback. *Remember, no feedback* is a type of feedback. If an employee never receives feedback on their performance, they will assume everything they are doing is working well or that their manager and employer don't care enough about them and their career to take the time to provide feedback.

How to Give Constructive Feedback to a High-Performing Employee

It is the dream of every manager to have a high-performing employee on their team. A high-performing employee is one who always gets their work completed to a high quality, is mature, and takes initiative to find their own answers. You might think that high performers don't need any type of feedback other than an occasional "Good job." High performers may not have obvious development or improvement needs, and we don't want to appear nitpicky when someone is doing a good job. In this way, finding quality constructive feedback for this type of employee can be even more challenging, so I will offer some considerations for conducting feedback conversations with high performers.

High-performing employees become frustrated when they ask for feedback and get the F-word: "Fine." It sounds like this: An employee asks their manager for feedback. "How am I doing?" And their manager responds with "You're doing fine."

High performers are not motivated by "fine." They want to be better than they were yesterday. I get that, as a manager, it can be challenging to come up with quality feedback for someone who consistently performs exceptionally. Feedback doesn't have to be about what they need to improve.

Feedback for a high performer can and should be about helping them move from *good* to *great*. It might sound like this: "Your presentation to the board last week was great. You are a natural presenter. If you are interested, we could get you some advanced training on how to be a high-impact presenter, if that is a skill you want to keep improving."

High-performing employees will not be satisfied to take on more work just because they can handle a heavy workload. Especially if they are picking up the slack for an underperformer on the team. The best gift you can give a high performer is to ensure you don't burn them out by expecting them to carry a heavy workload just because they can. The second-best gift you can give a high performer is to ask them if there is an area of their career they want to work on and improve to bolster their own career and make sure they are not carrying the load for other team members simply because you do not want to deliver constructive feedback.

FEEDBACK MISTAKES TO AVOID

Companies can support the wrong behavior in their employees and managers without realizing it by reinforcing and encouraging the use of outdated management practices.

The Feedback Sandwich

In the 1980s and '90s, it was commonly advised and recommended in management and communication training to "sandwich" constructive feedback or bad news between two pieces of positive information. "You are good at staying on top of deadlines. You need to do a better job of sharing information with your colleagues. I really value your ability to stay organized."

This structure for delivering feedback or bad news is also known as the *shit sandwich* or the *no sandwich*. This is *not* a sandwich you should ever serve to your employees.

The problem with this method for delivering constructive feedback is that something will be lost. The employee will either *only* hear the positive and not hear or improve on the constructive aspect or they will *only* hear the constructive aspect and not feel good about what they are doing well. I recommend having separate conversations for constructive and positive feedback to ensure the employee receives full benefit from each type of feedback.

I once had a client who attempted to fire an employee. The CEO and the COO spent so much time wrapping the termination in positive comments about the employee, they did not realize they were being terminated. They returned to work the next day with a thank-you card for the two executives. You can't make these stories up. This organization didn't have an HR adviser on their team, as you likely would have guessed. But they do now, after I pointed out to them the issues with letting an employee go without the proper support and processes in place.

Sandwiching feedback or bad news makes a manager look

insecure. It sends a message to the employee that you are unsure about the feedback you are delivering and there is no clear message as to how and why they need to change their performance. The entire conversation will feel like a confusing contradiction. The employee is likely thinking, "I am doing something right but also something wrong. So, what do you want me to do now exactly?" Employees can become confused as to what performance they should change.

Saving Up Feedback for the Yearly Performance Review

Another common mistake managers and organizations make is saving up feedback for the yearly performance review. Holding on to feedback, positive or constructive, for a yearly meeting is problematic for several reasons. Managers and organizations leave opportunities on the table to boost performance and engagement when they do not take the time to cultivate a feedback culture. If feedback is only given once a year in a performance review, a company has missed out on 364 opportunities to improve performance and provide recognition. (OK, we don't work 365 days a year, but you get the point!) Second, just imagine how the employee feels when they realize they have been making a mistake or underperforming for a while and no one told them. Not to mention how unsettling it is to receive a lot of constructive feedback at the same time in one meeting. Obviously, this is not a morale booster. Saving up feedback for the yearly performance review will not only hurt the career of the employee and manager but also affect productivity, profits, and employee engagement.

Blaming and Shaming

Opening up a constructive-feedback conversation with a shame or blame statement will certainly lead to a feedback fiasco. These types of statements sound like "You blew it in that sales meeting. Don't you know better than to talk over the client?" Or slightly less harsh, "When I arrived at the sales meeting, I realized you had packed the wrong handouts for me. This can't happen again."

Starting a conversation off with an accusation or indignity will result in negative feelings, will damage the relationship, and the person receiving the feedback will likely get defensive. We all make mistakes, and good managers approach performance issues and mistakes with a mindset of curiosity. They don't assume an employee is incompetent and recognize that a mistake or slip in performance is not a moral defect. Here is what giving an employee the benefit of the doubt with a curiosity mindset sounds like: "I noticed you missed the deadline for submitting your report this month. That's not like you, handing in something late. Is everything OK?"

Beginning a statement from a place of curiosity and giving the employee the benefit of the doubt will open the conversation instead of shutting it down. Giving someone a chance to explain builds trust. Delivering constructive feedback with the purpose of understanding what is going on for that employee at that moment presents a learning opportunity and helps them build on what they already know.

I Am Just Being Honest

Being direct with an employee about their performance is not a free pass to be a jerk nor is it justification for "brutal honesty." There is no excuse for being cruel, and statements that begin with phrases like "No offense but . . ." are unlikely to get a conversation off on the right foot. Typically, when a manager communicates in this way, it is a sign of a lack of self-awareness or at the extreme end, narcissism.

Every manager must strike a balance of being direct and kind while never sugarcoating feedback. A manager can be direct with what is expected from an employee while connecting that desired behavior to the employee's existing talent. In her book *Radical Candor*, Kim Scott describes this balance as "candor with caring"—after experiencing her own feedback fiasco of firing an employee without ever giving him feedback on his underperformance. (Spoiler alert: it didn't go well.)

Interrogate Your Processes Before You Interrogate Your People

I advise managers to take a diagnostic approach to performance issues to ensure they stay away from judgment and blame. This approach involves distinguishing between people performance problems and process issues. Countless workplace problems stem from deficient internal processes, often mistaken for individual performance issues. While some experts argue all problems boil down to process flaws, I know most stem from a blend of process and leadership challenges.

The "interrogate your processes" method involves investigating the root cause of a problem before addressing it with an employee. For instance, missed deadlines may seem like a people issue, but investigation might reveal flaws in project team setup or inefficient meeting structures.

A valuable tool for root cause analysis is the "5 Whys" technique, widely used in fields like engineering and safety. It involves asking "Why?" repeatedly to explore the underlying causes of a problem. For instance, if an employee fails to seek help when encountering work problems, the process could be examined:

> **Why isn't the employee meeting expectations?**
> **Answer:** There was a lack of clear guidance on what to do when facing obstacles.
> **Why wasn't clear guidance provided?**
> **Answer:** I assumed the employee would ask, but they felt hesitant due to my workload.
> **Why am I too busy to provide guidance?**
> **Answer:** Insufficient delegation and overestimation of employee skills.
> **Why am I not delegating effectively or assessing skills?**

> **Answer:** Feeling overwhelmed leads me to handle tasks myself, neglecting proper assessment.
> **Why am I stuck in this pattern?**
> **Answer:** I am stuck in delegating disappointment (go back and read chapter 3!). I need more support from my manager to manage my workload.
>
> Getting to the root cause of an issue may not require asking why five times, or it may require asking why ten times. The point is to take the time to get to the root cause whenever something isn't getting done to your satisfaction to solve a problem once and for all. Otherwise, we run the risk of treating the symptom, not the disease.
>
> Rather than hastily labeling employees as lazy or incompetent, managers must consider their own communication, management style, and organizational practices. A thorough evaluation of all contributing factors—managerial performance, team dynamics, and company culture—is essential to understand each employee's performance puzzle.

HOW TO ACCEPT FEEDBACK

Modern managers understand the importance of leading by example. If a manager expects an employee to accept constructive feedback without getting defensive or reactive, then it is essential a manager responds to feedback or issues in a mature, emotionally intelligent manner.

Constructive feedback was delivered top-down in the old-school corporate model. A manager or executive could deliver feedback to an employee, but employees rarely had an opportunity to express concerns or give feedback to their manager. Today's people-first companies understand that feedback can and should flow in all directions. A fast-growth tech company client of mine utilizes performance management software to ensure employees and managers can give and request constructive feedback on a regular basis. My client leveraged this software to reinforce a culture of consistent multidirectional feedback right from their start-up phase, and they are still using it today. Employees want a voice and to be heard. Fostering a feedback culture will improve manager effectiveness and employee engagement.

I made an attempt to discuss an issue with my manager once about a comment she made about me in a team meeting. I was upset and felt like my manager had basically called me incompetent in front of our entire team. I brought up the comment to her in a one-on-one meeting and told her how I was affected by her words. I was completely shocked again when she looked at me and said, "I think you're just being oversensitive."

My manager dismissed my feelings and my experience and labeled me because she didn't want to own up to her own behavior. The entire situation left me feeling like I could not trust my manager. We were able to maintain a professional working relationship but, as you would expect, I began looking for another role.

Even if you don't agree with an employee's assessment of a situation, never dismiss their issues or label them as oversensitive, dramatic, or anything else. Denial, dismissal, and labeling demonstrate a lack of empathy and accountability. This type of reaction will erode trust in the relationship. Labeling an employee as "too sensitive" because they refuse to tolerate a rude, aggressive, or bullying coworker is gaslighting and a form of incivility in and of itself. Remember, if you are labeling someone as "sensitive," you must be willing to consider if you are insensitive.

Knowing how to conduct constructive conversations, deal with conflict, and have difficult discussions is a management skill set that is just as important as knowing how to read a profit and loss statement. Yet training in these skills is often only requested when incivility or other issues have gotten out of control in a workplace. You can show someone respect and empathy even when you disagree with their experience or perception of a situation.

EMPATHY IS AN ESSENTIAL SKILL FOR MANAGERS

Empathy is the number one quality employees want from their manager, and it is a quality critical for maintaining relationships. Employees appreciate managers who care for them, both professionally and personally.

Yet there are days when it can be challenging to remember to slow down in our conversations with colleagues and team members to ensure we don't respond in a way that sounds dismissive. And as a habit, some people simply brush over people's comments about how they feel or what they are going through.

I have witnessed many conversations, for instance, where a stressed client or business associate had their experience and feelings dismissed by someone else in a meeting. During one stressful December I was on back-to-back Zoom meetings with various project teams and clients. Many of the meeting attendees, including me, expressed how we were feeling regarding our various stressors—deadlines, Christmas, the ongoing pandemic. And every time, I heard comments such as "Don't feel that way" or "You're fine."

Granted, in the moment it can be hard to come up with the most empathetic response. I don't think anyone realizes they are being dismissive and coming across as insensitive. I, too, am guilty of not always acknowledging someone's feelings as I push through a meeting or an encounter.

Nobody is perfect, but the good news is that empathy is more than an intrinsic quality only some people possess—it is also a skill you can develop, a muscle you can build with the right exercises and coaching. And if you want to be a great manager, you must develop it. Empathy is "the action of understanding, being aware of, being sensitive to, and vicariously experiencing the feelings, thoughts, and experience of another."[12] You do not always have to experience the same feeling as your employee or colleague to acknowledge their feelings or experiences with care and compassion.

How should we respond to employees or colleagues during a difficult situation or conversation? We can start here:

- Relating instead of dismissing. "I have definitely had moments when I felt that way."

- Getting curious instead of glossing over. "How might we make this easier on you?"
- Coaching instead of forcing. "Here's what I envision. How about you tell me how we can make this work."

Practicing empathy in nonwork situations when the stakes are lower is a useful exercise too. For instance, when in line at the grocery store, the person behind you comments about the price of groceries. This is an opportunity to respond in a way that lets the person know you heard them and understand the pain they are experiencing by saying something like "I know what you mean. My grocery bill has doubled." A dismissive comment might sound like "Yeah, but what can we do about it?" Even if a larger grocery bill is not affecting you, demonstrating empathy is a human response. No one wants their experiences or feelings dismissed. *We all want to be seen and heard.*

For managers, it's even more important to respond with empathy because it is what will build trust with your team members. And trust is an essential component of effective teams. I once worked with an executive who had empathy for anyone on their team who was going through a divorce. Because they had been through a divorce. They would give their team member as much time off as they needed. They had zero empathy, however, for anyone who was sick. Sick employees were expected to work through it.

If we are truly practicing empathy, we don't get to decide which situations we will empathize with. You may not have been through what your team member or colleague is going through, and you may not understand what it's like for them. But we can listen, acknowledge, and support the person.

If your team members are not responding well to your feedback, or your conversations in general, it is time to look at your communication style. I have coached many managers who are quick to blame the employee when a relationship isn't going well.

There are several other grave offenses of communication that managers must be aware of, as they only serve to disengage employees:

- using sarcasm to get a point across or point out a mistake
- only focusing on the employee's mistakes
- not listening and cutting off the employee when they speak

Every interaction with an employee is a chance to engage them and let them know you care. During stressful and busy times, it's common to default to bad communication habits. Managers must be extra mindful of how they interact with their team because of the influence their own mood and tone has on others. To navigate feedback or a difficult conversation effectively, we must slow down our own thoughts and emotions so that we can hold on to our humanity as we try to get the work done while really hearing what the other person is saying. Listening well is hardest when your thoughts and emotions are pushing you to make sure your voice is being heard.

There are techniques a manager can use to slow down

during a tough conversation so they can respond with intention and empathy. The next time you find yourself engaged in a tough conversation with an employee, slow down the internal chatter and flood of emotion by taking a deep belly breath and channeling your curiosity. Try to drop your assumptions about the other person's motives and leave blame out of the conversation. Asking clarifying questions such as "Can you tell me more about how you understand this situation?" will let the employee know you are staying curious and open.

CLOSE THE FEEDBACK LOOP

Have you ever left a meeting thinking everyone knows what action items they are responsible for, only to find in the next meeting that no one did what they were supposed to because it wasn't clear who was responsible for each action item? Even when a manager and an employee engage in a constructive-feedback conversation and the conversation itself seems to go well, it can still result in a feedback fiasco. The reason is often because the manager and employee did not close the feedback loop.

Closing the feedback loop means the manager and employee decide on the next steps and the metrics for evaluating improvement *before* the conversation ends, and there is verbal agreement on next steps. This is especially important when the feedback is constructive. If someone is putting themselves out there by initiating a feedback conversation, it would be a shame to see that effort go to waste because this critical final step was missed.

Here are some examples of how to close the feedback loop:

- "So to clarify what we decided—you will add your deadlines to your calendar, and we will review them every two weeks in our 1:1 meeting."
- "Can you send me the action items we agreed on today, and I will set up reminders in both our calendars to follow up on each one two weeks from now?"
- And my favorite question that I firmly believe should be used to end every meeting, "Who will do what and by when?"

We are all busy and want to make sure the time spent in conversations and meetings is useful and effective. Using any of these "close the loop" statements will ensure everyone leaves the conversation on the same page.

Constructive feedback should be given as soon as you notice an issue or see an opportunity for improvement. For example, if an employee's attitude is a source of frustration for the rest of the team, you need to have a feedback conversation with the employee as soon as possible. Allowing negative or disruptive behavior to go unchecked will erode the team culture, and the poor performance will eventually bleed over into the performance of other team members.

As Brené Brown once said, "Clear is kind." Leaving employees in the dark about their performance is unkind and unhelpful. Clear, specific feedback is like having someone turn on a light for us when we are sitting in the dark. Suddenly, we see ourselves and our work with more clarity. No one can improve their performance without feedback, yet few managers and employees effectively deliver and accept it.

Knowing how to deliver effective, actionable feedback is an essential skill for a modern manager. Awareness of an issue is the first step in making an improvement. A good employee will want feedback so they can attain new heights in their career. Another essential skill and tool you will need to bring out the best performance from your team members is coaching. Incorporating the coach approach into feedback conversations is an effective way to help an employee discover their own potential.

END-OF-CHAPTER REFLECTION, EXERCISES, AND TOOLS:

1. Reflect on a feedback conversation between you and an employee or colleague that didn't go well. Why do you think it didn't go well? What could you have done differently, even in beginning the conversation? Being more specific and less subjective about the results you were looking for?
2. Have you ever used the feedback sandwich when delivering feedback? Has anyone used the feedback sandwich on you? Do you see how "sandwiching" expectations or feedback can be confusing for some people?
3. Have you ever delivered constructive feedback in a direct message or an email when the information probably would have been better delivered in person? How will you manage the fear of delivering constructive feedback next time so you can have a better conversation in person?

CHAPTER 5

Frustration #4—Coaching Confusion: Why Most Managers Think They Are Coaching When They Are Not

Coaching is a transformative process between two people, the coach and coachee, that can result in a subtle mindset shift or a detailed action plan to work toward change. In the context of a coaching conversation between a manager and employee, the manager asks open-ended questions to help the employee uncover their own answers or solutions. Coaching is about helping someone learn rather than teaching them. Coaching is different from other conversations because the manager does not provide the answers or feedback directly but instead asks questions to help the employee unlock their own potential.

In their Project Oxygen, Google discovered that their employees ranked coaching on top as the most important competency they want their managers to have. Gallup's book *It's the Manager* (2019) shares: "If leaders were to prioritize one action, Gallup recommends that they equip managers to become coaches" for the coming decade.

The International Coaching Federation research from 2019 on "building a culture of coaching" shares that organizations with a strong culture of coaching are twice as likely to be high-performing.

Becoming a good coaching manager takes practice. The following scenario captures the struggle many managers have when they try to use the "coach approach" with an employee.

>**Sarah:** Alex, I've noticed that you've been having some challenges with your current project. Can you tell me what you think is causing the issues?
>
>**Alex:** Well, I'm not sure. This one just isn't going as smoothly, and I'm stuck.
>
>**Sarah:** OK, let's think about this together. Can you tell me what you believe your strengths are when it comes to this project?
>
>**Alex:** I guess . . . I'm good at following instructions?
>
>**Sarah:** That's a start, Alex. Now, what aspects of the project do you find most challenging?

Alex: Umm . . . I'm not sure. It's all kind of hard, you know?

Sarah: OK, let's try a different approach. Why did your other projects run more smoothly, and what do you think is the difference between those projects and this one?

Alex: Well, last month I completed that small project on my own, but this one is just different, I think.

Sarah: All right, we can work with that. What made you successful with the previous project?

Alex: I'm not sure, Sarah. It just felt easier, I guess.

Sarah: Alex, we need to identify the root of the problem here. Without knowing what's causing the issue, it's hard for me to guide you effectively. Bring me your project brief, and I will jump in and tell you where you need to go next.

Alex: OK. Here's the brief.

Sarah: Let's start by looking at the project requirements and any additional resources you might need. For this type of project, you really need a larger team to support you. Call Human Resources tomorrow and see if there is anyone available who could do a six-month secondment. Let's map out a plan for the first phase of the project right now and that should help with getting you started. Sound OK?

Alex: Yes.

Coaching is about asking the right questions, maintaining patience, and empowering employees to identify their own solutions. Sarah, however, seems to become impatient when Alex doesn't immediately identify why he is struggling with this project. Rather than ask more questions to help Alex get to the root cause of his issues with the project, she gives up and switches to manager mode, where she tells Alex what he must do to get the project on track.

This chapter will clarify everything managers need to know about coaching so they can use the coach approach effectively and avoid the frustration that comes with these common confusions. You will learn how to leverage coaching to empower your team to thrive.

WHAT IS THE REAL PROBLEM, AND WHY IS THIS FRUSTRATING?

Both the practice and business of coaching have become mainstream. The title of coach was once relegated to sports, but now anyone can obtain a coaching credential or take a workshop to learn how to take the coach approach to help someone else improve their performance or circumstances.

I have spent years obtaining my coaching credentials and have logged thousands of hours coaching leaders in a 1:1 format and training managers on how to take the coach approach with their team members. In my years as a leadership coach and in training others to coach, I have recognized that there is a great deal of confusion about what coaching is, which contributes to the frustration for managers.

This confusion can stem from several points:

- not understanding what it means to truly take the coach approach
- not knowing how to conduct a coaching conversation from start to finish
- not fully understanding when to coach and when not to coach

Let's define what coaching is once and for all, because many managers think they are coaching when they are not. Coaching, by definition, is a process of self-discovery and self-awareness whereby a coach asks open-ended questions to help the coachee unlock their own inner resources, which includes helping them find their own answers, next steps, values, strengths, and more.

There are many varied definitions out there on coaching. Some even use terms like *training* and *guidance*. But if you see a definition of coaching that includes these types of terms, know that this describes coaching in the broader sense of a multifaceted approach used to help develop someone.

True coaching is asking open-ended questions.

If you are telling, you are not coaching.

If you are training, you are not coaching.

If you are advising, you are not coaching.

If you are mentoring, you are not coaching.

All these development modalities are useful to help an employee realize their potential and solve problems. Each modality has a time and a place, and knowing when to leverage each one is crucial for the manager and the employee. The following table is a useful reference explaining different development modalities.

Coaching	Future-focused and solution-focused. Self-discovery from the person being coached. *Asking* open-ended questions to plan, problem-solve, or create awareness.
Counseling/Therapy	Focus on the past, present, and future. Focus on healing. A therapist can diagnose disorders and prescribe and facilitate treatment.
Mentoring	Mentor shares stories and experiences so the mentee can learn from them. Sometimes provides advice.
Training	"How to" and instructional focus. Some telling or asking.
Advising	Providing answers and making recommendations. Telling, not asking.

In any given conversation with an employee, a manager may need to train an employee on a new task (training), and the manager may share a story about their own experience (mentoring) and then ask open-ended questions to gauge how confident the employee is feeling about the work (coaching).

For many managers, coaching can and will be used on the spot as a development tool to help an employee shift their mindset or attitude to build awareness. In any conversation the manager may take the coach approach but, depending on the context, be required to switch to trainer or adviser mode. I call this *switching hats*. Switching between each development tool requires quickly identifying what is and is not a coaching moment between a manager and an employee.

TO COACH OR NOT TO COACH

Twelve years ago, I gave myself the gift of hiring a career coach. I was feeling lost in my career and needed some guidance on my next steps. My coach was phenomenal, and together we discovered that my next step was entrepreneurship. Fast-forward to the present day and I have my own thriving leadership coaching and training company. I was so moved by the impact of coaching I wanted to help others experience the same transformation.

As a leadership coach, I have witnessed my clients transform before my eyes. And because I have had the privilege of logging hundreds of hours coaching managers and business owners, I am also aware of when 1:1 leadership coaching is *not* the solution for improving a person's performance, mindset, or self-awareness. The coach approach can be used in many situations where a manager is attempting to support an employee, but not in *all* situations. It is important for any manager to be able to identify what *is* a coaching moment and what is *not* a coaching moment.

There is a simple technique that can help a manager understand if they should coach, train, mentor, or advise an employee in any given moment: the attitude, aptitude, or additional resources ("Triple A") framework.

When you are communicating with an employee and you are trying to support them or address a performance situation, you can ask yourself if the real problem is about attitude, aptitude, or additional resources.

- *Attitude* in the context of coaching refers to an employee's mindset, motivation level, or thoughts and beliefs about themselves, others, or their work.
- *Aptitude* refers to a person's capability, and in terms of employee performance it refers to their skill and knowledge level.
- *Additional resources* are for when you realize an employee is lacking the tangible resources they need to do their work.

If the problem is either of the latter two—aptitude or additional resources—it's unlikely you're seeing a coaching opportunity. If an employee is lacking in skill or knowledge (*aptitude*), this is a training opportunity, not a coaching opportunity, even if coaching may play a part later, with follow-up questions after training. And if it's an *additional resources* problem, the answer is to aim to provide the employee those resources they need to do their job well.

The only true coaching opportunity is regarding *attitude*. Coaching is all about shifting mindset and creating awareness that will lead to positive action and behavior change. It is time to leverage the coach approach when you notice an employee is struggling with the wrong mindset, thoughts, or beliefs about their work, or they are not aware of how a particular behavior is impeding their success.

Let's say an employee has been consistently late turning in their quarterly reports. You know the employee is aware of the deadline because you reminded them of the deadline the first time they were late with the report. You decide it's time to sit with the employee and inquire as to why they have been late with their reports.

If the employee responds with "I find our new accounting software to be confusing, and it is taking me longer to generate reports than it did with the past software," this is an *aptitude* problem. The employee requires more training or knowledge of the new system.

If the employee responds with "We have been short-staffed since Deborah left, and I am struggling to keep up with the increased workload," this is an *additional resources* problem. Hopefully you will be able to find an additional team member to take on the extra workload.

But let's say the employee responds with "I find this work of generating the same reports every quarter to be mundane. It's hard to get motivated to do them when I have so much other work to do." This is an *attitude* problem and therefore a coaching opportunity. The employee is struggling with their motivation, and they don't see the value of the task they are being asked to do. They also may not see the task as a priority, or their sense of being overwhelmed may be blocking their ability to self-motivate. As the manager of this employee, I would ask the employee what motivates them and what type of work they like to do. Based on their response, I would ask more questions to help the employee see a similar value in the work they don't like to do so they can learn how to shift their perspective about their work and better self-motivate.

FOSTERING SELF-AWARENESS

You can also use the coach approach to help someone build self-awareness around their performance if an employee is not aware of the impact they are having on others. Oftentimes this situation will call for a combination of feedback and the coach approach. We have all worked with people who consistently interrupt others in meetings to the annoyance of their coworkers. A manager might pull that team member aside, give them feedback, and ask them questions to gauge whether the employee realizes what they are doing. It might sound like this:

> **Manager:** Do you realize how often you interrupt your coworkers in meetings?
> **Employee:** No, actually I didn't.
> **Manager:** I am curious, why do you think you do that?
> **Employee:** I am always worried that if I don't get my idea or solution out in that moment, I will forget it.
> **Manager:** That's fair. I worry about that, too, sometimes. Do you think you could bring a notebook and jot the idea down so you don't forget it and then wait until a coworker is finished speaking?
> **Employee:** Yes, I can do that. I hope my coworkers aren't too annoyed with me.

This scenario has the manager using a coach approach to deliver feedback.

Sometimes, on the surface, it can look like an employee is struggling with embracing behavior that is considered important to be effective in their role. Taking a closer look, however, their manager may realize the employee is missing the skills and tools they need to handle a situation. For example, let's say a customer service employee didn't handle a difficult customer appropriately. It might be easy to assume the employee has a bad attitude or a temper and, therefore, this is a coaching moment (attitude and behavior). However, after speaking with the employee, the manager realizes the employee has never had training in how to deal with difficult customers or on how to navigate a difficult conversation.

There is a time to train and a time to coach. Training is for skills development, whereas coaching as a development tool is used to ensure employees have the right mindset, behaviors, motivation, perspective, and attitude.

If you feel that an employee requires more coaching than you are equipped to provide, you can absolutely hire an external professional coach or ask another manager in the organization who has more advanced coaching skills to assist in the employee's development. It is important, however, to recognize that an employee must *want* to be coached.

Companies will often approach me after I have delivered a talk or a session to the organization to ask me to coach their managers. Most managers sign up for 1:1 leadership coaching enthusiastically because most people like the idea of coaching. During their first couple of sessions, however, managers realize coaching includes accountability, and suddenly the allure of coaching disappears. One-on-one coaching is only effective when the coachee brings their full selves to the table and has bought in to coaching and the coaching process. If you are offering to coach an employee or hire an external coach to work with them, it is important that the employee understands what is involved in working with a coach and the expectations for how the employee will interact with the coach.

Sometimes, if an employee is struggling in their role and the offer to work with a coach has been made, they can feel pressured to agree to coaching. If you sense that an employee is not a willing participant in coaching, I recommend a different approach, such as group training or seminars. Group training and professional development programs can be highly effective in fostering self-awareness and helping an employee recognize how they may be showing up at work, without the pressure of focusing solely on their own behavior in that moment. Making a 1:1 coaching engagement mandatory for a manager or employee will affect the employee's experience and impression of coaching and may not lead to a positive result.

IS COACHING A TOOL FOR EVERYONE?

Coaching cannot solve all performance issues and is not right for every employee or manager. It is a proactive, future-focused development tool best used with individuals who demonstrate a willingness to improve and are motivated by personal growth. *Coachable* is a term used to describe someone who is open-minded, committed to their own growth, accepts feedback, and fully participates in a coaching conversation.

Even when a manager is clear on what coaching is and when to use it with an employee, the manager can still become frustrated when they ask open-ended coaching questions to an employee, only to find their employee is at a loss for answers or is simply unresponsive. When clients have been trained on the coach approach and are using it regularly with their team members, I often get an email or phone call from a frustrated manager stating, "I am asking open-ended questions, and the employee responds with 'I am not sure,' every time."

This can be frustrating for a manager who genuinely wants to help an employee build awareness and shift their mindset. Two things managers also need to know about coaching are that:

- not everyone is coachable; and
- not everyone is coachable by you.

The temptation is often to revert to telling an employee what to do. And I would never suggest leaving an employee hanging when they need an answer. Taking the coach approach is also not the "guess what's in my head" approach. So if an employee needs an answer, give it to them.

If, however, you are trying to coach an employee to come up with their own answer to a particular situation or to foster self-realization and the employee responds with "I'm not sure" or "I don't know," I suggest telling the employee to take some time to think about the situation and come back to you in a couple of days with some ideas.

A good employee is one who is willing to accept feedback and be coached, and is also willing to reflect on their own performance and communicate their professional needs. If an employee is not coachable you will often hear a lot of excuses from them, and they will rarely take responsibility for their own performance. However, an employee may be coachable, but their current manager may not be the right person to coach them. An effective coaching conversation requires enough trust for the person being coached to be vulnerable. It can be challenging to be vulnerable and admit your shortcomings to your own manager. The stakes may seem too high for the employee. If you suspect that an employee is uncomfortable being coached by you, it is a good idea to take the time required to build trust in the relationship before attempting to use the coach approach. One way to build trust is by sharing stories about mistakes you made in the past. A willingness to be vulnerable in front of your team will give your employees permission to be vulnerable also.

The key to effective coaching is to stay patient, ask probing questions, and guide the employee to discover answers themselves. For the person for whom coaching is not yet a fit, there are other development tools and strategies such as training, feedback conversations, advising, and mentoring that can be used to build work-related skills.

HOW TO STOP ADVISING AND START COACHING—WHAT QUESTIONS DO I ASK?

A tough habit to break as a manager is your desire to jump in and fix situations for your employees or team. We assume we are hired to be "fixers" and "advisers," and whereas these may be functions of your role, they can keep you from working on higher-level management tasks that only you can do. Plus, constant fixing and advising creates dependence, where employees are always relying on you for help. If you find it challenging to stop fixing and advising, remember that you are holding yourself and your employees back. Your employees cannot grow as professionals, and neither can you because your time and energy are being used up by putting out fires.

Coaching, on the other hand, is the ultimate tool to help employees make decisions and solve problems themselves. And that means managers properly become the off-ramp for the work, not the bottleneck. Coaching builds the confidence and independence employees need to rely less on their manager and continually take on more complex work.

So the next time you hear yourself offering a directive or solution to an employee, take a mindful moment to stop yourself and ask them an open-ended question instead. That question can be as simple as "What approach do you think you should take?" Give the employee the chance to think for themselves. If they don't have an answer, then you can provide it. Once managers realize the benefits of taking the coach approach, they begin worrying about what questions to ask to guide an employee to unlocking their own answers.

Coaching does not have to be complicated or take a long time in order to yield maximum impact. If you can stop yourself even once from *telling* and switch to *asking* an open-ended question, you are coaching. Imagine you are leaving a meeting with a team member who just bombed a presentation in front of stakeholders. The conversation might go like this:

> **Manager:** So, how do you think that went?
>
> **Employee:** OK, I guess. I think I could have done better.
>
> **Manager:** In what way?

Employee: I thought I knew my numbers, but when they started asking questions I got flustered and stumbled.

Manager: How do you think you can make sure that doesn't happen again?

Employee: I can practice my presentation more. I can work on managing my emotions in these presentations.

Manager: That sounds great. Are there ways I can support you to achieve this?

Employee: Yes, I think if you and I ran through the presentation beforehand, that could help.

Manager: Great, let's do that next time. In the meantime, don't be hard on yourself. These meetings are intense.

This is a perfect coaching conversation. In some instances, an employee may not be aware they did not do well, or worse, they don't really care. Here's how a coaching conversation might go with an employee who lacks awareness of their performance.

Manager: So, how do you think that went?

Employee: I think it went fine.

Manager: OK. Do you think there were parts of your presentation that weren't fine?

Employee: Not that I can think of. I got through it all.

Manager: Yes, you did. These meetings

and presentations are important for our stakeholders to decide if we require more resources for our organization. Are you open to some feedback on your presentation style?

Employee: Sure, I guess.

Manager: It seemed like you became flustered when asked questions about the Q4 financial performance. Typically, when you and I meet, you always know your numbers. I am curious: What happened?

Employee: Did it really sound like I didn't know my numbers? I didn't realize.

Manager: It's not so much that you sounded like you didn't know your numbers. It was more like you were taken off guard by the questions you were getting. It's easy to get so caught up in preparing for the presentation that we forget to plan for possible questions we might get.

Employee: Yeah, maybe. How do you know what questions you might get asked? How can you prepare for that?

Manager: Well, the first time I did one of these presentations I was surprised by the volume of questions I received. I didn't realize that not everyone on the board has the same background as me, so they needed me to repeat some data that was in my presentation. After each presentation I would make notes on the types of questions I got and then I would adjust my presentation style to make it easier to understand. Eventually, I didn't get as many questions, but I was always prepared for the typical ones you get in every meeting.

Employee: That's a great strategy. I will start doing the same.

Manager: Great, and I will pass on my notes about the questions I would get. And we can practice together ahead of the next meeting.

In this coaching conversation, the manager uses the situation as an opportunity to give feedback. When the employee doesn't have awareness of how they delivered their presentation, the manager doesn't let it go. The manager pushes through and changes their approach. The manager does ask permission to give feedback, which is an effective strategy, delivers the feedback, and then switches back to coach approach by asking an open-ended question. The remainder of the conversation is more of a mentoring conversation with the manager sharing their experience and strategies.

In any conversation you have with an employee, you may be giving feedback, coaching, mentoring, and advising. Modern managers can switch modes based on what the employee requires in that moment. In the above scenario, the employee wasn't aware of the issue, so the manager went into feedback mode, then switched back to taking the coach approach, and then offered their own experience to help the employee. This scenario is more representative of an everyday encounter between a manager and an employee. Managers sometimes use the coach approach to help an employee become aware of their own performance issues. In most cases, a good employee would fix an issue if they were aware of it. This is when taking the coach approach may not get a manager the result they need. A combination of providing direct feedback with the coach approach and mentoring can be more effective.

Coaching was never intended to be used tactically with someone whose performance is not up to par. The person must first be made aware of the issue, and only then can the coach approach be used as a tool to help them unlock their own performance. I have witnessed managers trying to use the coach approach to make someone aware of a performance issue because they didn't want to provide direct feedback. The hope is that if they ask the right question, the employee will have a realization about their performance and the manager won't have to give the employee constructive feedback. This is another reason managers experience "coaching confusion." The coach approach was used as a form of avoidance rather than as a tool to unlock potential. Using the coach approach in combination with direct, constructive feedback is a more effective approach to ensuring an employee understands where they are going wrong and how to improve their performance.

> ### Powerful Coaching Questions
>
> Coaching works best when used as a proactive methodology with employees and managers who are coachable and already performing at a high level. Attempts

to use the coach approach on someone who does not want to be coached in that moment or is not coachable, or when it is not about helping someone unlock their own inner resources, will likely result in more coaching confusion. If you are the type of manager who likes to jump in and provide solutions for an employee but realize you are not doing your employees any favors by saving them, it can be helpful to keep a short list of questions nearby you can ask in the right moment.

Expansive questions to open the employee's perspective and problem-solving abilities:
- How do you feel about that?
- I am interested to hear what you think you should do.
- Can you tell me what you need right now?
- How can I best support you right now?

Clarifying questions to ensure the manager and employee are on the same page:
- What is the end goal?
- Can you provide more detail / be more specific?
- Can you say more about that?
- What is the part that is not yet clear?

Anticipation question to generate positive thoughts and feelings:

- What do you think is possible?
- What if it works out exactly as planned?
- What is exciting to you about this?
- What is your sense of urgency trying to tell you?

Learning and reflection questions to build competency:
- If you could do it over again, what would you do differently?
- How else might you handle a situation like that?
- What did you learn from this?
- What led up to this situation?

HOW TO BRING A COACHING CONVERSATION TO A CLOSE

Managers often encounter situations where they began a coaching conversation with an employee but don't know how to bring it to a close. Or they ask the employee open-ended questions, but the employee is unresponsive and responds with "I don't know."

Knowing where to take the conversation or how to bring the conversation to a close will become easier with experience. A good way to close a coaching conversation is to provide a recap of what was discussed and commit to next steps. I encourage all managers, executives, and business owners to ask the same question at the end of every meeting and conversation: "Who will do what, and by when?" It is a simple question that fosters accountability and keeps everyone on track. Another simple coaching question that can be used to close the conversation is "What is a next best step?" These questions encourage an action-oriented mindset since coaching is not just talking; it is meant to be solution- and action-focused. If you are attempting to coach an employee who is responding with "I am not sure," I suggest setting a goal such as researching options and meeting again in two weeks to discuss ideas. There is no point in letting a coaching conversation go on and on when the employee is not contributing to the conversation. A different development approach may be required.

LISTEN TO LEAD

A small thing you can do right now to be a better manager and coach is to truly listen when your team member is trying to have a conversation with you. One of the biggest issues I have heard about since we all moved to work-from-home arrangements is that managers are multitasking during one-on-ones with their team members. Meaning, while an employee is trying to talk to their manager, their manager is checking email or responding to Slack messages. People can tell when you are not engaged in the conversation. And they can tell when you are working instead of listening. Work-from-home is amazing, and we all want to keep it. But we can't allow uninspiring management habits to set in that will lead to disengagement. Remember, no manager ever listened their way out of a job.

Active listening[13] is a core competency for coaches. *Active listening* is defined as focusing on what the coachee is and is not saying to fully understand what is being communicated in the context of the coachee's reality. When you are actively listening to your employee, you will notice subtle changes in their body language, emotions, energy, and tone.

Active listening is a skill that fosters trusting and productive dialogue. It creates a balance between listening and sharing your thoughts when you're in conversation with another person with the intention of understanding. It will also deepen your understanding and connection. Practical applications of active listening include not interrupting the other person and waiting until they have completed their thoughts, as well as paraphrasing back what you heard to ensure you understand the true meaning of what the other person said. I wish I didn't have to say this, but glancing at your phone or smartwatch while the other person is talking is *not* active listening.

THE POWER OF ASKING GOOD QUESTIONS

One practice that will instantly boost the performance of any company is to encourage both managers and employees to build a habit of asking more questions. Managers who ask good questions during one-on-ones will be able to uncover issues faster *and* help team members grow and develop in every conversation. If an employee happens to have a manager or colleague who is not the best at delegating or communicating, knowing they can feel comfortable asking clarifying questions to get the information they need will help them perform more effectively. Asking more questions can feel awkward at first and may require some training, but eventually both manager and employee will communicate more effectively. Typically, the result is a better working relationship and improved productivity.

Using the coach approach does not mean that managers should no longer direct their teams, but rather that their management style becomes more adapted to a given situation and responds better to the needs of their team members. One of the most common "identity" issues that I have helped leaders overcome through coaching is the idea or mindset that, because you are in a leadership role, you must have all the answers. I get the pressure that comes with being in a leadership role and the need to mask any feelings or perceptions of incompetency. A leader's job, however, is to build an outstanding team so you are surrounded by people with the answers. Let your team members shine and have the spotlight for a few moments while they demonstrate their expertise. This approach builds trust, loyalty, and engagement and greatly reduces the pressure on you.

Coaching is a powerful tool for unlocking someone's potential and helping them find the motivation to make necessary changes to their performance. A deeper understanding of the different types of motivation will enable you to ask more effective coaching questions to spur an employee to even greater heights of performance and success without relying on carrots and sticks. Because let's face it—inspiring performance rather than having to be a driver of performance is better for everyone.

END-OF-CHAPTER REFLECTION, EXERCISES, AND TOOLS:

1. Have there been times when you thought you were coaching but you realize now you were training or advising an employee instead? What will you do differently next time in a similar situation?
2. Active listening is an essential skill when taking the coach approach. The next time your child, spouse, or friend is speaking, practice turning off the voice in your head that is formulating your response and truly listen to what they are saying. Ask follow-up questions to understand what they are saying. Paraphrase back to them what you think you heard. Were you correct?
3. Staying out of judgment is essential when taking the coach approach. Even when an employee is not coming around to an approach or answer you think is suitable, it is helpful to remember that everyone is doing the best they can with the tools they have. Practice staying out of judgment the next time someone shares a decision they made or an opinion.

CHAPTER 6

Frustration #5—Motivation Mismatch: How Do I Light a Fire in My Employees? (or the Answer to "No One Wants to Work Anymore")

One of the biggest shocks a new manager will experience after their first promotion is how much harder it is to motivate other people compared to sustaining self-motivation. As individual contributors, we are accustomed to only having to light a fire under ourselves to get things done. We might assign ourselves a deadline or plan on rewarding ourselves with a nice bottle of wine when the project is completed. But now we must light a fire *in others* and that is not so easy.

Here is a conversation I had with a client that captured this frustration:

> **Corina:** How have things been going with your team's performance? The last time we spoke, your company was implementing some morale boosters like an appreciation night with prizes. How did that go?
>
> **Mark:** Yeah, the company has put in a lot of effort lately hosting employee appreciation events, increasing the perks, benefits, you name it. I thought these incentives would motivate the team. Now I am not so sure they have been effective. It seems like the more we give, the more employees expect. I have heard some comments from team members that sounded like entitlement. And I have not seen any noticeable improvement in productivity and performance.
>
> **Corina:** That's a common misconception, Mark. These external perks are wonderful, but they often only scratch the surface. Tell me, what motivates you personally?
>
> **Mark:** Well, I like feeling connected to the bigger picture. When I feel that sense of accomplishment when we reach our team goals, I am motivated to do more. It's the feeling that what we do matters, you know?
>
> **Corina:** That's insightful, Mark. What about your team? Have you explored what

truly motivates them beyond the surface-level perks?

Mark: Now that you mention it, we haven't delved deeply into that. I mean, I assumed everyone would be thrilled by the perks, but maybe there's something more they're seeking.

Corina: Exactly. Often, intrinsic motivators like a sense of purpose, a clear vision, and a feeling of belonging are the driving forces. When employees feel connected to the bigger picture and understand how their contributions fit into the company's vision, that's where true motivation thrives.

Mark: It makes sense now. Perhaps we've been focusing too much on external rewards without nurturing that internal drive. But how do I shift this focus within the team?

Corina: You mentioned that you feel motivated by a sense of accomplishment and when your work is connected to the bigger picture. How might you do that for your team members?

Mark: I guess I could start by making sure my team knows the value of their work and the impact it has. If I create an environment where everyone feels their work is meaningful and valued, maybe they will be more motivated by a shared purpose.

Corina: That's a great place to start. When individuals see how their efforts contribute to a greater cause, that's where true motivation ignites. Have you conducted open discussions with each team member about their individual aspirations and how they relate to the team's goals?

Mark: No, but I can add that into our agenda for our one-on-ones each month. I can try to connect their personal motivations with the team's objectives, making it not just a job but a shared purpose. Thank you, Corina. This conversation has shed a new light on how I can approach motivating my team.

Corina: Absolutely. And to be clear, I am not saying "get rid of all perks." Keep the fun stuff and remember it's not just about the parties and perks; it's about nurturing a sense of purpose and vision within your team.

WHAT IS THE REAL PROBLEM, AND WHY IS THIS FRUSTRATING?

Some companies spend a great deal of resources trying to motivate employees. When companies do not understand what motivation is and where it comes from, they tend to rely on what I call the "3 P's" of motivation—perks, parties, and prizes. US businesses spend $176 billion per year to motivate and recognize their employees with perks and prizes such as award points, trips, gift cards, merchandise, and other external rewards.[14]

External rewards are important but will only go so far in

terms of engaging and motivating employees, yet some companies do not seem to make a connection as to why they spend money on material things and get the same level of performance and commitment. Companies and managers then get frustrated when they notice entitlement settles in among employees when they stop doling out parties and prizes.

This frustration for managers comes from several points:

- not understanding the difference between extrinsic and intrinsic motivation, and how and when to activate each type of motivation
- not recognizing that what motivates one person may not necessarily motivate another
- not talking to employees to find out what is really important to them about their work to understand what lights them up

Lasting motivation is deeply internal and specific to each individual employee. Something inside of each of us must be activated to get us moving and to get us to care. A motivation mismatch occurs when companies and managers do not recognize the importance of internal motivators and do not take the time to create a work environment that activates that internal fire.

WHAT IS MOTIVATION?

Motivation is the force driving us to act. There are two types of motivation, intrinsic and extrinsic. When action is driven by tangible external stimuli or outcomes, it is known as *extrinsic motivation*. When action is driven by internal drivers, it is known as *intrinsic motivation*, whereby the activity is perceived as its own outcome.[15]

Extrinsic motivators are external rewards such as money, perks, prizes, job titles, and praise. Intrinsic motivators are internal rewards that are intangible such as acknowledgment, feeling a sense of belonging, a sense of purpose, and relationships.

Six Seconds, an organization providing emotional intelligence training and resources, describes motivation using the iceberg metaphor: "At the tip of the iceberg are those visible, tangible activities, extrinsic motivators. Beneath the surface are the invisible, emotional drivers which shape attitude; the second category. These emotional drivers make a difference in how activities are done and thereby define the impact employees have on customers and colleagues." Extrinsic motivators drive external results, such as following procedures and showing up for work and doing the basic requirements. If you want above-and-beyond behavior such as commitment, innovation, and teamwork, then you must activate intrinsic motivators and tap into what is most important to each individual employee on your team. Once you understand the two different types of motivation and what type of performance is activated by each motivator, it becomes easier to light a fire *in* your employees, so you never have to light a fire *under* them.

HOW AND WHEN TO USE EACH TYPE OF MOTIVATION

There is a time to leverage extrinsic motivators. A sales manager in a successful family-owned car dealership attending my group program shared a story on how effective extrinsic motivators can be to achieve a certain type of performance. A big part of Liam's role is to motivate his sales team to move cars off the dealer lot and into the driveways of customers. During our discussion on motivation Liam mentioned that if there is a car that has been sitting on the dealer lot for a while, all he must do is add an additional $500 commission to the sale and the car will be sold by the end of the day. Liam also mentioned that the performance of his sales team will typically return to previous levels once there are no additional commissions to be had.

When short bursts of performance are required, extrinsic motivators can help employees to find the energy they need to get over the finish line. The problem with extrinsic motivators is that managers will need to find new or additional sources of reward to keep the energy going, which can get expensive. There is also a risk of entitlement setting in among employees who require more incentive to perform.

Sometimes, intrinsic and extrinsic motivators can be used together to create a more rewarding employee experience. When I was fresh out of university, I was working for an environmental laboratory that hired many new grads to work on the frontline processing samples. The pay was lousy, but you got to work with people your own age and it was a great "foot in the door." Each Wednesday, my department had to work late to catch up on the backlog of samples. We were the only department that ever had to work late, which could have been demoralizing. However, my colleagues and I didn't see it that way. We had the entire building to ourselves, which meant we could turn on music and organize ourselves how we wanted to get the work done. Our manager, who didn't stay late, would always come to us before he left for the day and give us his personal credit card. He would tell us that we had a budget of twenty dollars per person to order dinner.

Our manager did not have to buy us dinner. And I hope the company reimbursed him. But it was the gesture that kept us smiling and joking with each other while we worked. We had the entire cafeteria to ourselves as we ate our delivered food and got to know each other better. Technically, buying dinner is an extrinsic motivator, but the gesture activated a sense that our manager cared about us and encouraged team bonding, which serves as an intrinsic motivator.

Many companies will attempt to leverage the low-hanging fruit of motivation, extrinsic motivation, first by throwing money at the problem. They host lunches, parties, and dole out company merch. These things are great and can be effective in boosting morale. Extrinsic motivators do not last, so once a company starts handing out prizes and perks, they must keep the good times flowing to maintain motivation levels.

Intrinsic motivators ignite a feeling inside us. That feeling can be achieved in many ways, but one of the most effective intrinsic motivators I have witnessed is helping employees find a deep sense of purpose through their work. When employees become aware of the impact they are having and understand that they are doing more than filling a seat in the office, you will get a new level of commitment and performance. This can be accomplished by explaining the impact an employee's work has on the bigger goals of the company.

The hit TV show *The Bear* is a great example of how to leverage intrinsic motivation to change the performance of an underperforming employee. Richie, a.k.a. Cousin, is an underperforming, change-resistant employee with a bad attitude. The new restaurant owner, Carmen, is desperately trying to turn the establishment around, and Richie's performance will sink the ship if he doesn't step up. Carmen sends Richie to job shadow in one of the world's best restaurants. What Richie views as punishment turns into a lesson in excellence. When Richie observes the entire staff's commitment to "blowing someone's mind" each night, he finally understands what work is about—making a difference in someone's life. Richie completely changes his attitude and level of commitment.

An effective method for activating intrinsic motivation is to help employees understand the impact their work has on the life of someone else. Sharing positive feedback from customers and clients is one way to accomplish this. If your company does not get positive messages from happy customers, then you know you have work to do on your customer experience. You may have to paint an imaginary picture of what blowing someone's mind might look like until you get real results you can share with your team members.

UNCOVERING YOUR TEAM'S INTRINSIC MOTIVATORS

Personalized employee recognition can be an effective strategy for activating intrinsic motivation. The key to effective recognition is ensuring it is meaningful to the employee. Companies tend to approach recognition in the same way they approach motivation. They hope that one type of recognition will work for all employees. I still see companies using an Employee of the Month program and I cringe. These types of employee recognition initiatives are often based on popularity and can feel more like exclusion than inclusion.

According to a report conducted by Gallup and Workhuman, most employees want to know their efforts are noticed yet *only one in three workers in the US strongly agree that they received recognition or praise for doing good work in the past seven days.*[16] When those efforts are recognized in a way that is meaningful to the employee, you will have effectively activated a new level of intrinsic motivation.

There is a simple method any manager can use to find out what type of recognition will be meaningful to each team member. Each time you onboard a new employee to the company or your team, give them a "recognition questionnaire." The questionnaire asks the employee about their recognition preferences and captures a list of their favorites. On your questionnaire, ask each employee *how* they want to receive recognition. Do they want to be publicly or privately recognized? Some employees would love a shout-out on a company Slack channel, while other employees would be horrified to be singled out in front of others. A quiet, heartfelt thank-you would be appreciated instead. When I survey employees on behalf of a client, overwhelmingly the most common response is "I want a personalized thank-you from someone in management." You read that correctly. The most impactful form of recognition that will activate intrinsic motivation is a personalized thank-you from a manager. And that won't cost a company any money.

Specifically, this recognition is most effective when coming from a different, more senior manager than the employee's direct manager and it's personalized to communicate the specific impact it had on others. It might sound like "Hey, I just wanted you to know that I really appreciated it when you stayed late to help my team last week. You helped us meet our deadline and maintain customer service standards. It means a lot especially since it wasn't your team." Nearly one-quarter of employees surveyed in the Gallup report say the most memorable recognition comes from a high-level leader or CEO.

The second question on a recognition questionnaire that can help a manager personalize recognition is "What type of reward do you prefer?" You can provide a short list of options such as these:

- an extra day off this year
- lunch delivered
- a gift card to my favorite shop

You will need a budget for these types of rewards. You can also ask questions about an employee's favorite beverage or snack so you can surprise them with a treat occasionally. Snacks, beverages, and items such as gift cards are extrinsic rewards. Personalization, however, activates an intrinsic response.

These types of recognition are most memorable for employees:[17]

- public recognition or acknowledgment via an award, certificate, or commendation
- private recognition from a boss, peer, or customer
- receiving or obtaining a high level of achievement through evaluations or reviews

- promotion or increase in scope of work or responsibility to show trust
- monetary award such as a trip, prize, or pay increase
- personal satisfaction or pride in work[18]

As you can see, most of these memorable recognitions do not involve financial reward or compensation. Compensation does matter, but money alone does not motivate people to go above and beyond.

You can send this type of questionnaire to your current employees right now. You don't need to wait for a new employee to join your team to find out what is most important to your current team members in terms of recognition. According to Gallup, only 10 percent of employees report being asked about their preferences for how and how often they get recognition. Imagine how motivating it will be for your team members to receive a survey asking them how they want to be recognized. The survey alone is not enough. You must use the data to make recognition and rewards more meaningful and motivating.

Recognition Survey

When employee recognition is done correctly, employees are four times as likely to be actively engaged at work, and five times more likely to feel connected to their workplace culture.[19] For recognition to be effective, it must be meaningful and authentic. And the only way for it to be meaningful is to find out what type of recognition each employee will value.

The exact survey looks like this:

1. How do you want to be recognized by your manager or a colleague (public recognition or private, like a note)?
2. If you were to receive a token of appreciation, what would that look like for you (gift card to your fave place, tickets to an experience of choice, etc.)?

Employee preferences must be kept somewhere that a manager or colleague can access so they can recognize and appreciate each other in a way that the person being recognized will find meaningful.

Recognizing the hard work of your employees in a way that is meaningful to them will have a huge impact on employee engagement, retention, and productivity.

Employee recognition also has a positive impact on retention rates and performance. An employee who has been recognized is 63 percent more likely to stay at their current job. With this type of reported impact, it makes it even harder to understand why more companies are not implementing thoughtful recognition programs. Only 36 percent of employees report their organization having some sort of recognition system in place, and 40 percent of employed Americans feel that if they were recognized more often, they would put more energy into their work. This is clearly a missed opportunity for many companies, but that doesn't have to stop you from recognizing your employees today.[20]

Recognition is an important tool for managers because it is easier to inspire performance than be a driver of performance.

Also, the behavior that gets recognized gets repeated! About 92 percent of workers are more likely to repeat a specific action after the action is recognized.[21] Because employees are motivated to continue to do great work if they feel their contributions to the organization are noticed. We all know how it feels to be seen and for someone to notice how hard we are working. Make someone's day and recognize how they have gone above and beyond for you or someone else.

LEADERSHIP STYLES THAT IGNITE INTRINSIC MOTIVATORS

Few things will demotivate an employee as much as knowing their hard work is going unnoticed. They want to know their efforts mean something. And it is just as important to evaluate the factors that might block or deflate motivation. One thing that will block intrinsic motivation is having a manager who is not motivated to go above and beyond. The attitude of an employee's direct manager will inevitably affect the motivation of each team member.

I remember sitting in my first annual performance review with my manager. I was excited to talk about my performance and my career goals. I was shocked when my manager looked at me and said, "These reviews don't mean anything. It's just for HR and their records." I sank into the chair, deflated. All employees want to be seen and heard. They want their efforts noticed. Sometimes, performance reviews are the only opportunity employees get to discuss their performance and goals with their manager. So when my manager told me that our performance review didn't mean anything, I went back to my desk questioning what it was all for. Why was I working so hard? How would I ever get ahead or move up if performance reviews didn't mean anything?

Communicating and behaving in a way that will demotivate your team is like shooting yourself in the foot. You are working against yourself as you drain your team of energy and drive. Even if you don't see the benefit in something, it is important not to let your attitude and energy affect your team. There are different management styles, and some are more motivating than others. When it comes to management styles that demotivate, I have witnessed them all from my own managers throughout my career.

I worked for the "fun" manager who wanted to be everyone's friend and "one of the gang." I also worked for the manager with a poor work ethic who would proclaim "I am done" each day at 1:00 p.m. I worked for the micromanaging manager who was intimidated by my high performance and drive and did everything she could to hold me back. Obviously, none of these management styles were motivating to someone like me who can produce a high volume of high-quality work. If an employee was motivated by any of the styles I just described, they are not the type of employee you would want on your team.

The management style that will motivate most employees is a style called *lead by example*. Lead by example means the manager must go first and demonstrate the behavior and values they expect to see in everyone else. They must embody the level of performance and motivation they want to see in their team members. Energy and emotions are contagious. And the emotions and energy of a manager hold more weight because of the authority that comes with their role. Employees are looking to their manager each day to set the tone for how the team will work together and the quality of the work produced by the team.

This means if the manager doesn't care about the work, likely neither will the employees. If the manager can't accept feedback, neither will their employees. If the manager accepts poor performance from a team member, then that performance becomes an acceptable standard for the entire team. For any high-performing employee, few things are as demotivating as being a member of a team of underperformers.

One of the most inspiring leaders I ever met sends his team two-question surveys periodically to ask them what elements of his leadership style are working for them. He asked his team members: (1) What aspect of my leadership style is working for you?, and (2) What aspect of my leadership style is not working for you, or what needs to change? He printed the responses and posted them in his office for all employees to see. He kept doing the things that were working, and each week committed to improving the items employees said were not working.

I was commissioned by this manager's employer to write a leadership case study about him, so I asked his team members what they liked about him. His team sent me a massive list of their manager's best qualities. The list was so long I couldn't include most of the feedback in the case study. A manager who "walks the talk" and is completely transparent about their own results will inspire and motivate everyone around them.

MOTIVATING UNDERPERFORMING EMPLOYEES

On many occasions I hear "I just don't know how to motivate this employee" from a frustrated manager who is dealing with an underperforming employee. My process for helping a manager work with an underperforming employee begins with asking if the underperformance is an issue of skill or will.

Skill refers to evaluating whether the employee has been trained properly to be effective in their role, expectations have been communicated, and the employee has all the resources they need to do their role effectively. *Will* refers to the employee's level of self-motivation and work ethic. People have their own individual levels of self-motivation. Some people are highly self-motivated and don't need to rely on others or outside circumstances to motivate them to do their work. Others have a low level of self-motivation, are not ambitious, and therefore struggle to motivate themselves to work.

There is an old expression: "Never saddle a dead horse." The expression can be traced back to the world of horsemanship. The expression serves as a warning to not waste your time, effort, or resources on something that won't go anywhere. Metaphorically, the phrase suggests that we should not invest our energy into something that is already lifeless or doomed to fail. It urges us to recognize when a situation or project is no longer viable and to redirect our efforts toward more fruitful endeavors.

It may sound harsh or even disrespectful to refer to an

unmotivated employee as a "dead horse," but as a manager, your job is not to be a parent or professional motivator to your employees. As I mentioned, you can create the conditions for motivation and your employee has to meet you halfway by learning how to self-motivate and bring their best self to work.

The best way to deal with a "dead horse" is to never hire them in the first place. Screen for self-motivation in the interview. Look for a history of personal and professional endeavors that require high levels of self-motivation in the candidate's past. Ask questions in the interview about why they chose a certain path in life or their career. Listen for their level of personal motivation and ambition.

If you suspect you already have a "dead horse" on your team, it's time for a conversation with them. Ask them what they really want to do with their career and life. Some people just want a job, and that's fine. They may not be motivated by working hard to get a promotion or to advance their career. Expectations around performance and quality of work must be communicated to this employee and will likely have to be repeated. I also recommend hard deadlines to keep an unmotivated employee on track. As a manager, you must also decide what type of performer and person you want on your team.

MOTIVATING HIGH-PERFORMING EMPLOYEES

A company's success can be a result of the efforts of a small percentage of its workforce. These high performers regularly meet or exceed expectations and, at their best, bring the whole team to greater levels of achievement.

Growing up, I was the kid you didn't have to worry about. I

was the "good soldier," as my first leadership coach put it. I did what I knew needed to be done and didn't make a fuss about it. Self-sufficient children often grow up to become the high performers in the workplace. We are good employees who just get the work done. Companies love us because we are easy to "manage." The most frustrating aspect of my career, however, was when lower-performing colleagues were threatened by my performance.

Indeed, high performers and star players can often stand out on a team or in a department and become targets for the employees who don't want someone else making them look bad. High-performing employees want to work with other star players. They need recognition even when they say they are not working for the recognition. If the only reward for hard work is more work, then they will likely move on, because as adults, high performers know their value. High performers won't stick around to pull the weight of underperformers tolerated by management.

Companies spend a lot of resources trying to recruit the best talent yet put little thought into what it will take to motivate and retain those rock stars. Only 4 percent[22] of an average organization is made up of these super-engaged workers who not only perform at high levels themselves but also appear to spread their positive engagement and commitment to others. For that reason alone, companies must put effort into finding out what will motivate and engage high performers to ensure they stay at the company.

Everyone on a team will need something different to reach their fullest potential. Managers must be trained in how to respond to those different needs and motivators. As I mentioned, high performers don't just want more work to do. That is not a reward. They may, however, want the opportunity to work on something new that will help them build more mastery in their area of expertise and become known as an expert in that area. They also want a seat at the table to share their ideas and concerns. When management and leadership don't listen to their input or concerns, high performers will assume the company doesn't care about them or their success. Without recognition and opportunities to improve and grow, these employees will likely burn out or feel resentful.

High-performing employees are often vocal about their needs. It is simply a question of whether companies and their managers are listening. Some managers spend so much time supporting underperformers, they neglect the needs of their top performers. Assuming high performers are self-sufficient and do not need to be "managed" is a mistake since those employees also want to be supported and recognized, just in a different way.

INTRINSIC MOTIVATION AT THE COMPANY-CULTURE LEVEL

Sometimes a manager can do everything right when it comes to activating motivation in employees. The company they work for and its culture, however, seem to be working against them. Sometimes good employees don't leave managers, they leave a toxic culture. Workplace culture is the shared beliefs and values held by the entire organization. It is often referred to as *how we do things around here.*

How you do things around here will either motivate and inspire employees or have them questioning why they still work for you. For example, the words commonly used in your workplace create the vibe in your workplace and evoke emotion. So if you are hearing words and phrases like "It's Hump Day" and "TGIF," it is likely time to think about changing up the language, and therefore the vibe, in your workplace.

There are questions every manager can ask to evaluate whether the company culture is creating ideal conditions for motivating employees. Does your company have a clear mission, vision, and purpose that inspires? Is that mission, vision, and purpose communicated regularly to employees? Are the wins shared often and the losses viewed as learning opportunities? What is the language used most often at work and on Slack or Microsoft Teams messages? Do managers and executives speak in terms of problems and deficiencies and never about the opportunities? Are your employees competitive with each other, looking out for themselves, and often concerned about fairness?

Teams must be aligned by a common vision, mission, and purpose. A company's mission, vision, and purpose should never be treated as onetime strategic planning activity or fancy words on the website. Mission, vision, and purpose are tools essential to helping employees feel inspired by a common goal. It would be impossible for a company to design a workplace culture that activates all drivers of motivation in every employee. A well-articulated mission, vision, and values, however, will go a long way in inspiring current employees and attracting more talent.

You might be wondering what you can do to motivate your own team if your employer does not have some or any of the key components that will ignite employee motivation. If the company is not concerned about employee motivation, then why bother, right?

Yet it would still be in your best interest to take the initiative to uncover your own team's internal motivators. The recognition questionnaire, for example, requires a low amount of effort with a high return on investment. You will get greater commitment and performance from your team, making you more effective in your role. Whether you are a frontline or middle manager, you can also influence up and take the lead on suggesting it is time for the company to revisit its mission, vision, and company values. If your suggestions and attempt at influencing up are ineffective, you can still implement any of the strategies in this chapter to ignite the passion in your own team. Other managers and executives will likely notice and follow your lead, resulting in an improvement to the overall company culture.

THE CONNECTION BETWEEN MOTIVATION AND EMPLOYEE ENGAGEMENT

There has been a tremendous amount of research completed on employee engagement. I wrote my first book in 2017, *The Engaged Employee Blueprint,* because I could see that companies did not understand what it meant to engage employees, and unfortunately not a lot has changed. Engagement levels on a global scale have barely moved, with only about 33 percent of the US workplace and 23 percent globally[23] reporting they feel engaged or highly engaged at work. The good news is there is a correlation between the things that motivate an employee and the key drivers of employee engagement. The Conference

Board of Canada released their findings in 2017 on the key drivers of engagement in the Canadian workforce, and they discovered the following drivers:

1. Confidence in senior leadership
2. Relationship with manager
3. Interesting and challenging work
4. Professional and personal growth
5. Acknowledgment and recognition
6. Relationships with coworkers
7. Autonomy

What should be obvious from this research is that numbers 3–7 are also intrinsic motivators. So if companies and managers focused on creating the conditions for intrinsic motivation in their workplace, they would also likely have a highly engaged workplace.

Other research on employee engagement found that an employee's relationship with their manager is the number one driver of engagement. This is one of the key reasons I decided to focus my work on helping managers gain people-first leadership skills that will engage and inspire their team members. Fewer things affect the motivation and engagement of an employee than how they feel about their own manager.

WHEN MOTIVATION AND ENGAGEMENT ARE JUST NOT THERE

I have used the example of a past client, Michelle, to illustrate how to assess your management style to understand if it is affecting your employee's performance. After a conversation with her HR assistant Robert about his performance, Michelle noticed that Robert still seemed to struggle with motivation. Unless Michelle checked in with him frequently, Robert was unlikely to complete his work.

Michelle decided to make time in her schedule for a deeper, "gate opening" conversation with Robert to try to understand how he was motivated. She knew how to invite someone into a conversation from the difficult-conversations training she received in my Managing Made Easy™ program. In their next 1:1 meeting, Michelle took a more relaxed approach. Robert and Michelle usually talked about tasks and gave updates. This time, she told Robert she wanted to hear more about him and what he needed.

Michelle learned that Robert was still not feeling connected to his role. His past role, working directly with a local environmental group, had a lot of meaning and purpose, and completing paperwork at a desk was not enjoyable for him. He couldn't see how he was helping anyone by completing paperwork. The conversation lasted for two hours, and Michelle finally understood where Robert was coming from. She realized why he took the HR job—it was the safe career choice that his parents had always encouraged him to get. Robert's thinking was old-school. He was taught to believe that a person should get a good job, save money, and stick it out. Robert was fully planning on sticking it out in a job that did not light him up because it was the safe choice.

These conversations about motivation are ongoing between Robert and Michelle. Michelle has helped Robert see that you don't have to stay in a job you don't like simply because it is safe. She is also helping Robert see other career options available to him that could be a better choice. It will be up to Robert to decide what to do with his career. In the meantime, Michelle has set clear expectations for Robert as to the level of performance she expects from him going forward. She has also shared examples and stories about the impact his role has on the work lives of their employees at the organization to help him connect with the greater purpose in his role. According to Michelle, Robert's mindset has improved. In the past, he had a dark cloud around him and wasn't talking with her. Now, Robert is dropping by Michelle's office to chat, and he has a new comfort level with her.

Michelle has done her part. She has created a safe space for Robert to share his thoughts about his work and career so she can understand what motivates, or doesn't motivate, him. She has provided him with options for his career while also clearly communicating what she expects of him. The rest is up to Robert. He will have to find a way to self-motivate if he stays in a job that doesn't light him up or move on to a role in which he can find greater purpose and meaning.

It is not realistic for an employee or manager to be fully engaged at and with their work 100 percent of the time. We all have career ups and downs. Employee engagement isn't black or white. Employees are not either engaged or disengaged. Employee engagement levels are on a sliding scale, and employees can and will move up and down the scale during their journey with a company. Like motivation, the factors that lead one employee to become disengaged might not be the same for another employee. What's important is that we are tuned in enough to notice a drop in engagement levels in ourselves or our colleagues.

A great strategy that I picked up from an amazing leader is to initiate an "engagement conversation" when you notice a change in someone's (or your own) engagement level.

The conversation includes asking the employee (or yourself) two key questions:

1. What part of this (dis)engagement do I own?
2. What part of this (dis)engagement does the company / the manager own?

This strategy came from the amazing Jennifer Gillivan of the IWK Foundation, and you can read her full interview in my book *The Engaged Employee Blueprint*.

The further an employee slides down the engagement scale, the harder it is to pull them back. This is why consistently taking the pulse of your team makes it easier to spot when an employee is starting to slide in the wrong direction. For these reasons, every manager must have regular engagement conversations to find out where each team member is on that engagement scale and to understand the factors that are influencing their engagement or disengagement levels.

The way we talk about employee engagement is one of the reasons why the number has barely moved. When we talk about employee engagement, we talk about how a *company* must engage its employees. The problem with this is that only people can engage people. When we approach employee engagement from the viewpoint of a company engaging its workforce, once again companies often resort to one-size-fits-all attempts to engage employees using, you guessed it, perks, parties, and prizes.

When we acknowledge that true engagement is best achieved when people have meaningful interactions with each other, we realize we need to train and coach company managers on how to lead people. Every manager requires tools to uncover the individual drivers of motivators in team members and a willingness to get the most out of every interaction with team members.

A MANAGER WHO CARES

Empathy is an underutilized employee motivation and engagement strategy. The research on employee engagement and experience has proved that today's employees want a manager who cares about them. When I work with companies to improve employee engagement, we do tactical work—pulse surveys, diagnosing the issues, and I give managers practical tools for engaging their team. And managers and executives will learn that engaging and motivating a team is about the connection and emotional commitment an employee has to their work and employer. If an employee thinks their manager or employer doesn't care about them, it will be challenging for that employee to foster an emotional connection required to be engaged at work every day.

Managers (and companies) can demonstrate caring in their everyday interactions with employees by asking employees what they need to feel good about coming to work, getting creative to achieve organizational results without burning out employees, and having real conversations that leave the employee feeling heard.

Motivation is an inside job; therefore, to motivate a team

of employees, a manager will have to understand what is important to the people on that team. Managers will have to believe in their people and want them to succeed and reach their goals. I encourage you to reflect on your own internal motivations. Does the thought of helping others succeed light you up? How can you find more joy in developing others rather than feeling frustration when someone is not performing?

END-OF-CHAPTER REFLECTION, EXERCISES, AND TOOLS:

1. In the coming weeks, take time to go for a walk-and-talk or have a coffee with an employee. Without getting too personal, ask them questions about their past work experiences or their hobbies and activities as a child. Ask them why they made those choices (again, don't get too invasive). Their answers should provide some information into what drives them or what they are drawn toward.
2. Take notice of the work activities that motivate each of your team members in the coming weeks. How might you organize workloads so that team members are doing work that is motivating?
3. Consider if there is an employee on your team whose engagement level has decreased. Is it time to have a conversation with that team member about their engagement level? How might you address a decline in engagement with this person?

CONCLUSION

The Critical Path Forward for Managers

The most challenging aspect of my work is hearing the frustration in the voice of a struggling manager. They often beat themselves up over a mistake they made with an employee and start questioning whether they are cut out for management.

The most fulfilling part of my work is seeing the expression on a manager's face in one of my cohorts when they realize they are not alone and other managers are going through the same thing. Then, by the end of the first module, they realize there are tools, techniques, and skills they can learn in my program that will completely change how they interact and communicate with their team members and how they feel about their role as a manager. It is a combination of joy and relief on their faces as they realize they have been doing the best they can with the knowledge and tools they had, which in some cases was not a lot.

TURN FRUSTRATIONS INTO JOY

If you are a hardworking manager questioning whether you want to continue on a leadership path or return to being an individual performer, ask yourself:

- Have I received the appropriate type of management training for my role? (You will need different types of management and leadership development based on the type of role.)
- Was the training effective in helping me understand how to lead in today's workplace?
- Did I do my best to apply the learning each day at work with my team?
- Are there still gaps in my knowledge?
- Are my expectations realistic about what it will take to lead a team in today's complex, ever-changing workplace?

Overcoming the frustrations you experience each day requires several steps. First, make sure you have the training, knowledge, and tools you need to do your role effectively, typically obtained in a leadership development program designed for a modern people manager. If you have attended training, was it the type of training you needed, was it sufficient for your role, and were you able to apply what you learned when you returned to work?

Second, evaluate your own expectations. This step is more challenging than the first because we must be brutally honest with ourselves. In addition to setting expectations with employees, you must manage your own expectations as to how much effort is required to get to a place where you are working effectively with your team. Learning how to communicate with each other and work together effectively takes time.

Ask yourself how realistic your expectations are: Do you expect to delegate and walk away, and the work will get completed perfectly? It is possible to get to this place, but generally not the first time you delegate or begin working with your team. Did you expect that everyone on your team would be happy to have you as their manager? Hopefully your team already views you as a leader they want to work with, but there may be workplace politics at play, and you may have to deal with that before all your team members embrace you as their leader. Were you overwhelmed by the number of personal issues employees have brought to you since you became a manager? Each employee has their own comfort level with how much they will share with their manager. What is important to remember is that all employees have lives outside of work, and those personal issues can and will influence their ability to do their work. Part of your role as a manager in today's workplace is to support an employee's ability to balance work and life. You are not required to be a therapist or counselor for your employees, but you do need to know what resources are available that you can share with your employees when they need support.

Expectations are the root of all frustration. Asking yourself hard questions will ground your experience as a manager in reality. We imagine how something will go, and when it doesn't go that way, we become disenfranchised. We start asking ourselves, *Is this even worth it?*

Yet managers need not simply see every challenge as a frustration that makes the role "not worth it." Once a manager receives the right training and leadership development and has realistic expectations, they can finally tap into the *joy* that can come with leading others, including the satisfaction derived from tackling challenges rather than simply resenting them.

Rather than worrying whether asking an employee for an update is micromanaging, for instance, you can view the check-in as an opportunity to discover if the employee requires more support from you. Rather than getting frustrated with an employee's performance, you can view it as an opportunity to teach them, coach them, shift their mindset. Rather than secretly hoping a disgruntled team member will quit soon, you can see the situation as an opportunity to have conversations with them about what they really want to do with their life. You can be the manager who unlocks possibilities they hadn't been able to see for themselves.

CHOOSE THE RIGHT LEADERSHIP DEVELOPMENT FOR YOURSELF AND OTHER MANAGERS

Imagine you are a nurse, and you walk into the hospital for your shift only to be informed that, today, you are a doctor. Or imagine you are a bus driver, and you walk into work and are told that, today, you are the mechanic, not the driver. It would never happen. It is a different skill set requiring different tools, and even a different mindset.

Yet, as we know, companies are still promoting good employees to management without giving them the support and development they need. Some companies have not made the connection between effective management, employee productivity, and bottom-line results. They think leadership development is "nice to have" when time and resources allow. If you realize that you, or managers who report to you, could benefit from leadership development and need to make the case to your own manager, you can find a guide outlining the return on investment of leadership programming in the appendix. An old-school mentality that becoming a good manager is something that happens over time while on the job is another reason some companies may not invest in development programs. That is one part of the learning process, but managing effectively is also a learnable skill. A good management training program can shorten the learning curve for new managers and reduce the impact a first-time manager can have on the engagement and performance of their direct reports.

Modern managers need a "how to manage" program. Many companies make use of leadership development for managers. Not all leadership development is created equal, however. Training designed using a competency-based model that can be easily applied when a manager returns to work is more effective and will result in a higher ROI. Most leadership development programs leave managers with a massive amount of information to take back to work and figure out how to apply on their own. If you have attended leadership development but are still struggling with the people function of management, it could be that the development opportunity did not address your core needs. Learning needs assessments, cohort-based training, and a commitment to continuous learning are essential components of effective leadership development that will result in the highest-possible learning retention for the manager.

Cohort-Based Programming

For years, I delivered management and leadership development in a full-day, onetime format. Past participants from my sessions would approach me in the grocery store to say, "I just remember that one tool you gave us!" I recognize they meant it as a compliment, but I always felt somewhat defeated. I started realizing that if people could typically remember only one thing, then it was likely time for me to start teaching "one thing." Cohort-based learning is a more effective method for leadership development because participants learn and advance through the program together. Rather than attending a onetime full-day or multiday workshop, managers can return to work and apply what they learned in each session. They return to the same cohort to share their experience with their peers and continue learning core management skills. With remote work's rise, cohort-based management training is even more important. New managers once learned how to manage from observing colleagues and executives. If you and your colleagues work remotely, cohort-based group management programs can be invaluable for learning from peers and experts.

Assessing Learning Needs

The complexity of our work environments and the new

demands on managers necessitate a thoughtful approach to choosing leadership development. Companies often hire leadership coaches without considering whether managers lack fundamental skills that are typically obtained in a training program. It's crucial for technical-expert managers to first acquire essential leadership skills, for instance, in order to effectively address gaps.

Another error is the reactive use of leadership coaching. Coaching should be proactive, guiding managers from point A to B, and not used as a fix for poor performance or behavior. Feedback and tailored training based on management level are more effective approaches.

Ensuring all technical-expert-employee-turned-managers have mastered the fundamentals of leading a team will guarantee that the company (and its leaders) has a solid foundation for growth for years to come. Companies need a clear competency-based path for developing their leaders from emerging to executive because every stage of leadership will require a new set of skills and behaviors. Take a step back and assess the areas of management and leadership where you feel you struggle. Talking to a leadership coach can help you identify the type of training and coaching you need.

Continuous Learning

When it comes to improving performance, it is easier to go from good to great than from weak to strong. We know what happens when we don't take our car in for regular maintenance. The same is true for our own performance. Unlearning unhealthy management coping strategies is necessary to make space to learn the correct way to handle challenges and obstacles. Investing in the right leadership development program for you and your role will do more than just make you a better manager. It will ensure you stay resilient. Acquiring the skills and tools you need to be a modern manager can restore confidence and alleviate the five core frustrations.

Choosing the right leadership development for you or other managers is an important step, and choosing the right emerging leaders is also essential. All the management training and leadership development in the world cannot help a new manager who does not want to lead or deal with the "people stuff." For a comprehensive guide on how to choose the right leaders and how to support the transformation from technical expert to modern people manager, visit the appendix.

PREPARE YOURSELF FOR FUTURE DEMANDS

The demands, requirements, and expectations for managers are always increasing. As we learned in 2020, life is extremely unpredictable. Once, managers were only expected to manage the flow of work. Workplaces were policy-focused. Today, the best companies and managers are people-focused, and employees are looking for companies with a positive and supportive company culture first. The pace of change has accelerated, and managers are required to navigate increasing complexities. Therefore, a modern manager must be equipped with leadership tools to meet this demand. Companies are finally realizing they need to focus on diversity and inclusion. While this focus is long overdue, to build the kind of workplaces that are supportive for everyone will require managers to create an environment where employees feel seen, heard, and valued. This will come more easily to some managers than others. All managers, however, will need a certain level of support along with the proper tools to accomplish this. Companies are also facing pressure to act more sustainably and with greater social responsibility. Again, managers will need to learn how to lead a new model of business to prioritize people *and* the planet. And, of course, with remote and digital collaboration being the norm today and into the future, it is even more important for managers to understand how to bring a team together to work toward a common vision. Doing so in a remote setting will require sharp communication skills and relationship-building abilities to foster a sense of community in online teams.

Does your company have a clear path for supporting your managers and executives along their leadership journey? If an entire level of management in your company isn't thriving, is anyone thriving?

THE GIFT OF A GOOD WORK ETHIC

I worked with several less-than-effective managers throughout my career, and I am grateful for each one. They have taught me how *not* to lead. I am also grateful for the leaders and colleagues, formal and informal, I have encountered in my life who have taught me valuable lessons about how I want to show up in life and work. As I was building my career and developing my own work ethic in my twenties, I had a colleague who did not hesitate to pull me aside if they noticed I was not contributing to the team in the best way through my attitude or efforts. I did not always appreciate their feedback back then, but today I am grateful for the brave colleagues who invested in my growth. I have enough stories about lessons I learned from others in my career to fill another book. Those lessons helped me cultivate the work ethic and stamina I would need to start and grow a coaching company.

Every day I hear managers and business owners complain about "this generation." *They are lazy. They don't have any priorities.* My suggestion: rather than complaining about younger colleagues, give them the gift of a good work ethic. I have always been a hard worker, but it was these crucial lessons from others that helped me understand what it means to have the right work ethic. The next time you hear a complaint or a comment that demonstrates a lack of understanding about what is important at work, take the opportunity to create a learning moment. Find the courage to take that person aside and share an example or wisdom about why this work is important. This takes time and energy, but we can't blame a younger generation for their attitude if no one has invested in them. Manage your frustrations so you can lead by example.

BECOMING A MODERN MANAGER

I received a DM from a frontline manager who attended my fifth cohort of Managing Made Easy™ two months after the cohort ended. Her words were dripping with excitement: "I just received my first performance review as a manager and one of my team members said I was the best manager they ever had!" I was so happy for her, and it was like a proud parent moment for me. Each time I receive a frantic email or call from a frustrated manager, I tell them about that message. It is possible to enjoy the people side of management, even excel at it. The journey to becoming and remaining a modern manager is marked by self-reflection, learning, and a shift in perspective. Moving from the frustration of dealing with "people problems" toward the joy that comes from helping others develop and grow becomes possible when we shift how we see our role. You are not just a manager. Some days you are a trainer or a coach; other days you might be a facilitator of results. Other times you may be working with your own team as a collaborator for success. Once you have the right tools for your role, you get to decide what type of manager you want to be based on your employees' evolving needs. If, however, you dwell on the problems, you will always be frustrated and on the brink of burnout.

You are probably wondering where you will find the time to be this type of manager. Think instead: How much time will I ultimately save when my team is coming to me with fewer questions? You will spend less time and energy worrying about the difficult conversations, and you will jump in and begin the conversation. You will spend less time taking the work back and doing it yourself because you realize how long it will take to support an employee to become competent, and you have the tools to get there. You can find additional tools and training and coaching opportunities on my website at www.shiftpd.com. The path of managing people will often bring up doubts and challenges as you grapple with your own limitations and the complexities of leading others. Yet through the right training and development, coupled with realistic expectations, you can transcend these frustrations to lead by example and inspire the next generation of leaders. Sharing this book with your colleagues when you hear them express the frustrations you once had will create a shift within your entire organization; a shift toward modern people management will have employees and managers excited to arrive at work each day. Training all managers in your organization on the modern management principles and strategies outlined in this book will lead to a people-first workplace culture. By investing in continuous learning and fostering a culture of support and development, both managers and their organizations can thrive amid the ever-changing demands of the modern workplace.

Appendix A

FILLING THE LEADERSHIP PIPELINE FROM WITHIN: HOW TO TRANSFORM YOUR TECHNICAL EXPERTS INTO PEOPLE LEADERS

For years, the advice coming from management consultants and leadership coaches related to building a strong leadership bench inside a company was "Don't promote your best technical employees. You will lose a good employee and gain a bad manager." Sadly, I once even gave this advice. For today's fast-growth technology and knowledge-based companies, this advice is not helpful for several reasons.

The reality for today's workplace is that the company is growing, and someone must step up and lead the team. Most often, it will be the strongest technical person who is asked to lead the team because they already know the work and the team, and they can train and guide new team members. Vetting and hiring managers from the outside will take time, and most companies today want to move fast.

The second reason why this is bad advice is because it is unfair to hold an employee back from taking a leadership role simply because they are a strong technical performer and their manager doesn't want to lose them. After all, 45 percent of millennials say that a job that accelerates their professional or career development is very important to them.[24] If a company holds back their strong technical performers from advancing, they will likely lose good employees to companies that have a clear leadership and career development path.

So, how can technology and knowledge-based companies build a leadership pipeline from within using their strongest technical players? Decisions regarding management promotions are critical for businesses. Companies fail to promote the right candidates over 80 percent of the time—and promoting the wrong people into management costs organizations billions of dollars each year.[25] A more effective strategy for any company is to ensure all managers are getting the type of leadership development they need to succeed at every level of management. Each level of leadership will come with its own demands and challenges. This means frontline, midlevel, and senior managers who began their career as technical experts will require different types of training and coaching at each stage to develop their people skills and succeed in that role.

My experience as a leadership coach who has worked with hundreds of managers tells me that the first leadership transition from technical-expert employee to frontline manager is often the toughest leadership transition to navigate. Companies need a clear leadership development path that starts with supporting their expert individual performers in developing their people-leadership abilities to build a strong foundation for future leadership roles. In the sections below, I will outline what that leadership development must include to effectively transform technical experts into people leaders, how to gain buy-in from technical experts to embrace the "people stuff," and the common pitfalls all companies must watch out for when seeking out leadership development.

WHAT TO LOOK FOR IN TECHNICAL EXPERTS WHEN FILLING THE LEADERSHIP PIPELINE

Many employees get promoted to team lead or supervisor out of necessity. The company is growing, teams are adding new people, and the team needs an official leader. It's often the strongest technical person who gets promoted because of a "halo effect," where it's assumed that their strong expertise and technical ability means they will also be competent as a team leader.

I advise the companies I work with to go beyond strong expertise and technical ability and try to spot other characteristics and skills that would make someone a good manager. These characteristics include good communication skills, empathy, a natural ability to coach and bring out the best in others, and most importantly, ensuring that any technical-expert employee being considered for promotion to management is *coachable*. It is rare for any expert employee to transform into an effective people leader organically over time. Training and coaching are essential to support the transformation from expert employee to engaging people manager, so this one attribute of being coachable cannot be overlooked when trying to spot an emerging leader.

HOW TO SUPPORT THE TRANSFORMATION FROM TECHNICAL EXPERT TO EMERGING LEADER

Once a technical rock star has been identified as having leadership potential and is officially promoted to their first management role, it is important to get them enrolled in management training where they can begin building a foundation of people-leadership skills as quickly as possible. This type of training includes topics such as communicating expectations, how to delegate, delivering feedback, coaching "on the spot," and navigating difficult conversations. The sooner a new technical-expert manager builds a toolbox with these essential tools, the faster they will get comfortable and confident embracing the people side of a management role.

In the past, most management and leadership development programs were designed around learning *about* management. Effective management training happens when managers learn *how* to do management functions such as giving feedback and delegating effectively. For example, my program for frontline managers takes six months to complete because managers learn one skill each month and have time to go back to work and apply their new skill. They return to the next module and have time to discuss their challenges and celebrate their wins.

Because every stage of leadership will require a new set of skills and behaviors, companies need a clear path for developing their leaders from emerging to executive level. With a solid foundation built in the first stage through group training, once promoted to midlevel manager, training in topics such as managing other managers, team dynamics, emotional intelligence, and managing up and across is essential.

Once a former technical expert reaches senior management, I recommend working one-on-one with a leadership coach to further develop the leadership behaviors and mindset necessary to navigate complexity, adapt to change, and become the kind of strategic thinker typically encountered as senior leader.

Technical-expert managers face diverse challenges along each stage of the leadership journey; therefore, leadership development may also require a certain level of customization to be effective in preparing managers to overcome specific challenges at each stage.

As an example, a new technical-expert-employee-turned-manager in my group program for frontline managers embraced learning the skills in each module. The feedback from her team, however, indicated that while she was delivering feedback and delegating as she learned in the program, she still lacked empathy in her communication, especially if a deadline was missed. Many of the technical teams she was a part of as an individual performer believed that direct communication was essential to getting the work done. Because her manager was also trained by me to make note of where their frontline managers were strong and where they needed to develop, I was alerted to this issue and was able to work with the new manager to help her understand that a manager's communication style requires more consideration and tact because of how employees take in communication and feedback from their manager versus a peer.

HOW TO HELP TECHNICAL-EXPERT MANAGERS EMBRACE THE PEOPLE SIDE OF LEADING A TEAM

Companies should also expect that some technical experts who move into a management role may be content to lead the technical work but will not embrace the "people side" of leading a team. After all, that's not what they studied and trained for!

When a client of mine who is a senior technical manager in a production-design firm was struggling to let go of the technical side of the work, it was a colleague who pulled him aside to give him some "radical candor" about his management style. My client thought he was successfully managing a project team by running around and managing the technical aspects of the project when, in fact, he was preventing his junior team leads from learning the nuances of leading a complex, interdepartmental project by doing everything himself.

The feedback of "the project can't progress at the rate of you" was direct and delivered with caring as my client's colleague reminded him that his own career would also be stalled if he didn't pass his knowledge on to junior leaders and embrace the people side of leading a team.

Working with a leadership coach can help managers open their eyes to their blind spots. A technical-expert-employee-turned-manager who is struggling with delegating and knowledge sharing will also need to hear candid feedback in real time from peers they trust. Receiving feedback from different sources can help a "reluctant to delegate" technical manager realize the impact they are having on the progress of the team, the company, and their own career. Hearing similar feedback from different people means this feedback was not just one person's perspective.

Another way to get ahead of situations where newly promoted expert team leads might struggle to let go of the technical work is to set and reset expectations early about the management style required to effectively scale. Giving away your job, so to speak, is a necessary component for scaling a company—especially fast-growth tech companies. Cementing this expectation as part of the company culture can help technical-expert managers understand the importance of letting go of the work and passing on their knowledge to the emerging leaders behind them.

When working with adults, it is also important to connect new learning and expectations to their current knowledge. New technical-expert managers can be reminded that the skills they use to collaborate on technical work—such as communicating required changes to a design or troubleshooting a software bug—are the same skills they need to initiate and conduct performance conversations with an employee. Instead of designing new software, they are designing how a group of people can work together to bring an idea to life. New managers often just need someone to help them realize they already have a foundation for building their people-leadership skills.

FEEDBACK AND MENTORING MUST BE INCLUDED IN ANY LEADERSHIP DEVELOPMENT STRATEGY

As mentioned previously, a process for ensuring all new and experienced managers receive feedback from their direct reports, their own manager, and their peers is critical to developing managers at every level in a company. Feedback for new technical-expert managers shouldn't come only from their own manager; feedback should be delivered up, across, and down in the spirit of growth and development. Receiving real-time feedback from their own team members can help technical-expert managers understand the impact their management style is having on their team. Receiving consistent feedback throughout the year, not just once a year in performance reviews, will also allow managers to adjust their approach and self-correct before negative management habits become ingrained and then must be unlearned. Many of my clients are using performance management software that is prepopulated with feedback questions and is designed to appeal to technical-expert employees and managers.

Peer mentoring is also an important leadership development tool for technology and knowledge-based industries. Employees working in tech and knowledge-based companies are accustomed to learning with and from their peers to build their technical know-how. I encourage companies to create leadership communities of practice (Slack channels are a great place to start) where managers at all levels meet regularly to discuss the challenges and wins they experience in leading a team.

COMMON MISTAKES MADE WHEN CHOOSING LEADERSHIP DEVELOPMENT

One of the biggest mistakes companies make in terms of leadership development is arbitrarily deciding what leadership development a manager will need without considering the real learning needs of each manager. Some companies will look to hire a leadership coach to work 1:1 with a technical-expert manager who is experiencing issues with the people side of leading their team when that manager hasn't yet attended management training.

On the surface it can look like a manager is struggling with embracing leadership behaviors such as inspiring the best possible performance from their team. What is often the issue, however, is that the manager has not been properly trained on skills such as giving effective and useful feedback or coaching an employee on the spot.

There is a time to train and a time to coach. Training is for skills development, whereas coaching as a development tool is best used to ensure managers have the right mindset, behaviors, perspective, and sense of purpose.

While all managers can benefit from working one-on-one with a leadership coach, it's better for a technical-expert manager to gain the skills they need to lead a team first. Once a manager develops the skills they need to lead a team, it is much easier to know if that manager is struggling with the people side of managing—such as avoiding initiating feedback or career conversations with direct reports—or was simply lacking in the actual know-how to navigate these conversations.

The longer a manager is in their role without proper training, the greater the likelihood that they will develop negative management habits based on *coping* instead of *thriving*. It also increases the chances they will pass on bad habits to newer managers they may be mentoring. The reality I see daily in my group management programs is that not long after we begin the first session, the managers in the room begin to feel bad about how they have been leading their team. They realize there was so much they didn't know and now feel the embarrassment of how they handled certain situations with their direct reports. Ensuing all technical-expert-employee-turned-managers have mastered the fundamentals of leading a team will guarantee that the company (and its leaders) has a *solid* foundation for growth for years to come.

Appendix B

MAKING THE CASE FOR LEADERSHIP DEVELOPMENT

In today's postpandemic workplace, managers face unprecedented demands and pressures. Frontline supervisors and middle managers must balance multiple priorities, often with minimal support and recognition. Employee expectations are also shifting, placing new strain on managers. Amid these complexities, the importance of examining and enhancing management development strategies becomes increasingly apparent.

Leadership development is particularly crucial for first-time managers, many of whom are promoted based on technical expertise rather than managerial acumen. The transition to a leadership role can be fraught with challenges, including heightened stress levels and diminished team morale. Equipping first-time managers with the opportunity to acquire foundational leadership development on topics such as delegation, feedback conversations, coaching, difficult conversations, and employee motivation can support emerging leaders to navigate complex organizational dynamics and drive team success.

For managers grappling with familiar challenges such as competing priorities and decision-making uncertainties, leadership development offers a pathway to growth and effectiveness. When managers have the skills they need to lead a team, they are able to mitigate burnout risks in themselves and direct reports while fostering employee engagement at the same time.

THE BOTTOM-LINE IMPACT OF LEADERSHIP DEVELOPMENT

Research consistently underscores the pivotal role of top-performing managers in organizational success. Organizations led by such managers yield significantly higher total shareholder returns compared to those with average or below-average managers. There is a clear link between effective management and financial performance. Expecting managers to grow into a top performer without the required support, training, and development, however, is unrealistic and will result in a frustrated workforce.

A survey uncovered a noteworthy return on investment of $7 for every $1 invested in leadership development initiatives.[26] The survey further revealed that the average tangible benefit of leadership development initiatives across all participating companies amounted to a staggering $374,796,036. The median expenditure on leadership development stood at $1 million, equating to about $444 per individual.

Companies that invest in leadership development often experience better alignment with organizational strategies and a more robust pipeline of leaders available for critical roles. This strategic approach not only reduces stress among managers but also enhances organizational agility and resilience in the face of evolving challenges.

Talent attraction and retention is another key factor that must be considered to understand the true value of leadership development. Despite apprehensions and misunderstandings surrounding the ROI of training and development initiatives, the costs of neglecting employee growth are significant. Beyond financial returns, investing in training and development fosters employee loyalty, engagement, and productivity. Managers who feel valued and supported are more likely to remain committed to their roles and contribute meaningfully to organizational success. Investing in training and development also enhances organizational reputation as an employer of choice. By demonstrating a commitment to employee growth and advancement, companies attract and retain top talent, positioning themselves as leaders in talent development and retention.

The case for leadership development is compelling and multifaceted. From driving financial performance to fostering employee engagement and retention, the benefits are undeniable. By investing in the growth and development of managers, companies not only bolster their bottom line but also cultivate a culture of continuous learning and innovation, ensuring sustained success in today's dynamic business landscape.

Notes

INTRODUCTION

1. Jack Zenger, "We Wait Too Long to Train Our Leaders," *Harvard Business Review*, December 17, 2012, https://hbr.org/2012/12/why-do-we-wait-so-long-to-trai.
2. Employee engagement is the involvement and enthusiasm of employees in both their work and workplace. Jim Harter, "In New Workplace, U.S. Employee Engagement Stagnates," Gallup *Workplace*, January 23, 2024, https://www.gallup.com/workplace/608675/new-workplace-employee-engagement-stagnates.aspx.

CHAPTER 1

3. Dana Wilkie, "The Miserable Middle Managers," SHRM, February 19, 2020, https://www.shrm.org/topics-tools/news/employee-relations/miserable-middle-managers.
4. "The Squeezed Middle: Millennial Managers Worse-Off while Supporting a Burnt-Out Workforce," MetLife, September 17, 2021, https://www.metlife.com/about-us/newsroom/2021/september/the-squeezed-middle--millennial-managers-worse-off-while-supporting-a-burnt-out-workforce/.
5. "Mental Health at Work," World Health Organization, September 28, 2022, https://www.who.int/news-room/fact-sheets/detail/mental-health-at-work.
6. *Telus Mental Health Index*, Telus Health, January 2024, https://go.telushealth.com/hubfs/MHI%202024/Canada_MHI_January_English_2024.pdf.
7. Richard Fry, "Millennials Are the Largest Generation in the U.S. Labor Force," Pew Research Center, April 11, 2018, https://www.pewresearch.org/short-reads/2018/04/11/millennials-largest-generation-us-labor-force/.

CHAPTER 2

8   Richard D. White, "The Micromanagement Disease: Symptoms, Diagnosis, and Cure," *Public Personnel Management* 39, no. 1 (Spr 2010) 71–76.

CHAPTER 3

9   "RACI," Project Management Institute, https://www.projectmanagement.com/wikis/234008/raci#_=_.

CHAPTER 4

10 "Statistics on the Importance of Employee Feedback," Workleap blog, October 7, 2014, https://workleap.com/blog/infographic-employee-feedback/.
11 Denise McLain and Bailey Nelson, "How Effective Feedback Fuels Performance," Gallup *Workplace*, January 1, 2022, https://www.gallup.com/workplace/357764/fast-feedback-fuels-performance.aspx.
12 *Merriam-Webster*, s.v. "empathy (n.)," https://www.merriam-webster.com/dictionary/empathy.

CHAPTER 5

13 "ICF Core Competencies," International Coaching Federation, https://coachingfederation.org/credentials-and-standards/core-competencies#:~:text=Active%20Listening%E2%80%94Ability%20to%20focus,to%20support%20client%20self%2Dexpression.

CHAPTER 6

14 U.S. Businesses Spend $176 Billion on Incentives, Recognition, Rewards, Incentive Travel and Corporate Gifting New Incentive Market Study Shows," Incentive Marketing Association, https://www.incentivemarketing.org/IMA/News/Industry_News_and_Press_Releases/2022/US-Businesses-Spend-176-Billion-on-Incentives.aspx.
15 Laurel S. Morris et al., "On What Motivates Us: A Detailed Review of Intrinsic v. Extrinsic Motivation," *Psychological Medicine* 52, no. 10 (July 7, 2022): 1801–1816, https://doi.org/10.1017/S0033291722001611.

16 "The Importance of Employee Recognition: Low Cost, High Impact," Gallup *Workplace*, June 28, 2016; updated January 12, 2024, https://www.gallup.com/workplace/236441/employee-recognition-low-cost-high-impact.aspx.

17 "The Importance of Employee Recognition: Low Cost, High Impact," Gallup *Workplace*, June 28, 2016; updated January 12, 2024, https://www.gallup.com/workplace/236441/employee-recognition-low-cost-high-impact.aspx.

18 "The Importance of Employee Recognition: Low Cost, High Impact," Gallup *Workplace*, June 28, 2016; updated January 12, 2024, https://www.gallup.com/workplace/236441/employee-recognition-low-cost-high-impact.aspx.

19 Emily Lorenz, "Is Your Industry Delivering on Employee Recognition?," Gallup *Workplace*, September 13, 2020, https://www.gallup.com/workplace/400907/industry-delivering-employee-recognition.aspx.

20 *Empowering Workplace Culture Through Recognition*, Gallup *Workplace* and Workhuman, https://www.gallup.com/analytics/472658/workplace-recognition-research.aspx.

21 *Empowering Workplace Culture Through Recognition*, Gallup *Workplace* and Workhuman, https://www.gallup.com/analytics/472658/workplace-recognition-research.aspx.

22 Aaron De Smet et al., "Some Employees Are Destroying Value. Others Are Building It. Do You Know the Difference?," McKinsey & Company, September 11, 2023, https://www.mckinsey.com/capabilities/people-and-organizational-performance/our-insights/some-employees-are-destroying-value-others-are-building-it-do-you-know-the-difference.

23 "Employee Engagement," Gallup, https://www.gallup.com/394373/indicator-employee-engagement.aspx.

APPENDIX A

24 Annamarie Mann and Amy Adkins, "What Star Employees Want," Gallup *Workplace*, https://www.gallup.com/workplace/231767/star-employees.aspx#:~:text=Millennials%20are%20much%20more%20likely,18%25%20of%20baby%20boomers).

25 Randall J. Beck and Jim Harter, "Why Great Managers Are So Rare," Gallup *Workplace*, https://www.gallup.com/workplace/231593/why-great-managers-rare.aspx.

APPENDIX B

26 Wendy Hanson, "Leadership Development Programs Are a Quantified Profit Multiplier—Here's the Proof," *HR Daily Investor,* November 16, 2023, https://hrdailyadvisor.blr.com/2023/11/16/leadership-development-programs-are-a-quantified-profit-multiplier-heres-the-proof/.

About the Author

Photo © Alex Stead

Corina Walsh is a speaker, author, podcaster, and certified leadership coach on a mission to ensure all employees love going to work each day! Corina's programs leverage the transformative power of impactful leadership coaching, equipping managers and business owners with the fundamental skills and knowledge they need to excel in their roles and creating a ripple effect of positive change within organizations.

Corina's flagship program, Managing Made Easy™, has been delivered in workplaces in more than fifteen industries. Her innovative approach to leadership development has earned her many acknowledgments, including being named a Top 50 Leader Under 40 in *Atlantic Canada* and receiving a YWCA Woman of Distinction Award in Business.

ABOUT THE AUTHOR

As an international speaker on leadership and employee engagement, Corina has been included on speaker rosters with such dynamic experts as Brené Brown and Adam Grant. Corina is also the author of *The Engaged Employee Blueprint* and host of the podcast *The People and Culture Success Show*.